CRACK 'DA CODE

What Every College Student Needs To Know About Money, Love and the Dream Job

Sanyika Calloway Boyce

CRACK 'DA CODE
What Every College Student Needs To Know
About Money, Love and the Dream Job

Smart Concepts Books Publishing
28 Vesey Street, Suite 2266, New York, NY 10007

Published by arrangement with Smart Concepts Books and
SCB Publishing.

Library of Congress Control Number: 2003093237

ISBN: 0-9726320-0-X

Printed in the U.S.A.

---

*This book is available at quantity
discounts for bulk purchases.
For information, call (866) 4DA-CODE
or visit www.4dacode.com*

Table of Contents

DEDICATION

To The Rose Of Sharon, who introduced me to my best friend and true love. You are more special to me than I have ever been able to express, I pray I make you proud.

SPECIAL ACKNOWLEDGEMENTS

I must first thank God for His promise and faithfulness. My life has been a race of sorts and I am grateful that there was always someone waiting as the baton was passed.

Mommy & Daddy — I love you. Thank you for the gift of life.

Darrell — You are my cheerleader, my husband, my partner, and my friend. Thank you does not come close to expressing my gratitude. All I can say is, "You . . . you're good, you."

Maria — Everyone deserves a Mom like you. Thank you for being you.

Grandma Jones — Here's a little something to add to your collection. "Sendin' love your way."

Grandma Helen — Thanks for making me feel like part of the family.

Keesha, Ephraim, Shekinah, Quinton, CreVonte, Manna and Tyler — You inspire me to live my best life. Thanks for your prayers.

Rhonda — My sister, my friend. From ninth grade to now, we've come a long way, baby. Thanks for making the journey fun.

To all who have blessed my life with love, wisdom, and kindness, I hope you know how special you are to me. Thank you for your support and belief in me:

Jean Watson-Jeffery, Morgan Lambert, Wanda Brockington, Cheryl Walker-Robertson, Carole I. Smith, Clayton Banks, James Brown, Marjorie Billingsley, Linda Moffat, Opal Evans, Lucy Ryans-Raoof, Tina Redwood, Tim Sanders, Asha Tyson,

James Malinchak, Jerry Gant, my NAMIC family, Mr. Brown, Lisa Jones, Bonnie Chirigos, Earl Rodney Holman, my Showtime family, Kathy Moody, Andrea Fairweather, Dalilah Glenn, Evangel Church, Melvin Sykes, Chris Trinka.

If I've missed anyone, please forgive me.

To my Prayer Warriors: Rhonda, Paula and Bev — Monday mornings aren't the same without you. May God bless each of you exceedingly, abundantly more than you can imagine. Thanks for standing in the gap for me.

To the Girrrls: Oneeka, Bernie and Ebony — Here's to looking cute while being broke, barbecues, birthday dinners, weddings, new homes, growing up gracefully, and the future. It's gonna be bright; get your shades!

To my NSU crew: Eric, Zeeke, Patrick, Tony, Ericka, Ms. B, Dr. Tickton, Ms. Briggs, Dr. James, Mr. Opfer, Stacie & Jason, Karla, Kim, and Jada — This book would not have been possible without the experience. And the experience was made memorable because you played a part. Mass. Comm. rules! NSU . . . I love it, I love it, I love it!

To my R&D team: Kathy, Paula, Patrick, Mrs. Brockington, Alisa, and Louie — Thanks for reading the manuscript and making me believe in the possibility of a book!

To my advisors, mentors and guides: Ramon Williamson, Alex Carroll, David Ledoux, and James Malinchak — Through this process your passion for the challenge inspires me to press on.

To my editor: Donna R. Cornelius at WriteWorks (www.writeworksagency.com) — God sent you just when I needed your talent, your advice, and most of all your encouragement. Thank you for listening!

ADVANCE PRAISE FOR CRACK 'DA CODE...

Sanyika has "cracked 'da code," and college students (and their parents) should buy this book now! This dynamic young woman has candidly written a down to earth book that should be required reading for all young adults regardless of their academic status. Debtco's mission is to help individuals achieve a debt-free lifestyle in less than 3-years, but, by reading this book, students will be less likely to need our services! Surprisingly that makes us support the book even more!

Eric Porter
Founding Partner/Board of Directors – Debtco, Inc.

"Knowledge is power and *Crack 'Da Code* delivers muscle to college students (and their parents too!). This joyous read not only gives the reader insight, it contains Sanyika's spirit and essence divine. Give it a spin.

Tim Sanders, Chief Solutions Office, Yahoo!

Sanyika has "cracked 'da code" with this book. The information has solid content. With each page you will find fresh insight with real take-home value!

Asha Tyson, National Best-selling author of "How I Retired At 26!"

Your knowledge of the financial plight of college students is immensely helpful to promote positive student development.

Art R. Malloy, Associate Vice Chancellor for Student Affairs, Winston-Salem State University

College students need this information!

Rob Dixon, WHOV 88.1 FM, Hampton University

FOREWORD

Shauntay Hinton, Miss USA® 2002

Financial responsibility is never on your list of things to learn when starting college. Choosing a major, social activities, and being on your own inundate your mind when walking past credit card booths promoting all of their benefits and none of their hidden trappings. It all seems so simple, so harmless. Like millions of other students, I was unknowingly sucked in . . . uninformed.

I learned some of my hardest lessons about money at Howard University. I got into serious credit card debt that I am still paying for now. Had I read CRACK 'DA CODE then I would have had the tips on how to be more financially aware and would be without the "credit card debt monkey" on my back.

The information about money is detailed, easy to follow, and written in a language that is neither boring nor condescending. Its suggestions will help you set goals in all aspects of your life.

The decisions you make today greatly impact your future ability to buy a car, get a mortgage, obtain credit, and even get the job you deserve and desire. Take personal accountability for your actions. Read CRACK 'DA CODE: What Every College Student Needs To Know About Money, Love and the Dream Job.

Shauntay Hinton — Miss USA® 2002

P.S. It's the perfect gift for high school graduates heading off to college!

DISCLAIMER

The information presented in this book is correct and factual to the best of the authors and publishers knowledge, however its accuracy is not guaranteed and therefore, the reader should seek professional advice regarding matters discussed herein.

This public notice allows SCB Enterprise, hereafter referred to as SCBE and Smart Concept Books Publishing, hereafter referred to as SCB Publishing, to engage in a topic with regard to opinions relating to information contained within. SCBE and SCB Publishing intend for this publication to neither extend legal or financial planning nor take any other professional advisory position.

As publisher, SCB Publishing must also disclaim any personal liabilities that may occur due to your own actions, interpretations or negligence.

INTRODUCTION

I speak to thousands of students each year on numerous college campuses. One thing that continues to amaze me about the college curriculum is that most campuses don't offer a course on the importance of using credit in a responsible manner. If I were the President of a college I would never permit any student to graduate without passing this course.

When I received my first credit card in college, I thought someone had just given me $1,000. Little did I realize after spending all of it, that I would have to repay the money. To make matters worse, I was charged interest. This meant I would have to repay more than the $1,000 I had spent. I could have easily avoided getting myself into financial trouble had there simply been a college course that educated me about the importance of using credit in a responsible manner.

I'll bet your campus probably doesn't offer a similar course, either. However, the course is offered to you in *Crack 'Da Code*. This book should be mandatory reading for *every* college student in America and these strategies should be taught at *every* college. Sanyika Calloway Boyce shares simple strategies to avoid financial disaster while helping you to create a successful future. I wish I read this book when I was in college.

Read, absorb and follow the strategies in this book. This may be the most important book you ever read while in college!

James Malinchak — Contributing Editor,
"Chicken Soup for the College Soul"® and Author,
"From College to the Real World"™
www.Malinchak.com

PREFACE

My journey on the path to financial fitness began with much anxiety and almost by accident. Upon graduation from college, I had all the hopes of a wonderful life ahead. With a degree in my hand, a dream job on my mind, and a pile of debt in my pocket — I started out in the world. However, my hopes of success quickly came to a halt as I discovered I was not ready for the real world.

I had no idea how the debt in my pocket would alter my life in such a dramatic way. I came from a school of thought that said, "You can't squeeze blood from a turnip." Basically speaking, if you don't have it, they (the creditors) can't get it. I had no idea that they indeed had a way of getting it (the money you owe), or at the least the ability to make life unbearable in the process.

I wasn't really trying to dodge those creditors to whom I owed a collective $15,000. I was simply putting them off for a minute. The idea was to land my dream job, make good money, pay all the old creditors, and maybe start fresh by getting a few new creditors. Thus, proving I was a good and responsible person and not the deadbeat I was made out to be.

As I stepped onto the path of financial fitness ready to make those dreams of career, money, and love a reality, I learned the truth; money does matter. It plays a big part in how others perceive you, whom and how you love, and the career you choose or are forced to choose.

This realization came after learning that I was not going to get my dream job. Not because I wasn't qualified, in fact, they loved me and wished they could make an exception to hire me. However, because I had made several bad decisions regarding my credit, it was impossible for me to get a job that came with an expense account and a credit card. I was devastated. No one warned me. I had no idea how far bad credit could reach, but I was about to find out.

As though the career blow wasn't enough to keep me on the straight and narrow path of finances, I continued to make unwise financial decisions:

1. Co-signing for a friend's car loan.

2. Trying to pay a "Credit Doctor" to wipe my credit report clean. I had the crazy idea that I would reapply for the job with my new information and all would be fine.

3. Getting taken by a consolidation scam. Always check with the Better Business Bureau when considering working with any lender or agency.

Finally I decided that the process of getting out of debt and becoming financially fit was up to me.

On the journey to new found freedom, I thought I was the only one in the world to mess things up so bad. But, as I walked the rough, sometimes confusing, and always interesting path of money, love, and finding the dream job, I came across many weary travelers. Other good people who'd made bad decisions.

I found out very quickly that there was no one book, tape, pill, or potion. But, it was a combination of information and techniques that worked. As with many things in life, common themes guide us and fundamental principles prevail.

"Crack 'Da Code, What Every College Student Needs To Know About Money, Love & The Dream Job" is a compilation of fundamental principals and the steps necessary to understand and embrace. It is a map to make it on the road from young adult to adulthood. As you read this book I hope the tips and techniques will become traveling companions on your personal journey.

It is my hope that you will use this book as an active workbook and journal. Grab a pencil and a highlighter; and make the most of your investment.

Financial Fitness Can Be Yours!

The journey to financial fitness, like many other good things in life, is ongoing and I daily strive to work at my goals and ultimate destination. Yet, as I continue down the path, I am thankful that God

> *Life is change. Growth is optional. Choose wisely.*
> *— Karen Kaiser Clark*

has called me to share my experiences and through this process I continue to grow.

Section A

CRACK 'DA CODE ON MONEY

More is written about money than any other topic covered. We are fascinated with money: how much we have, when we'll get more, and what we'll spend it on. Money is important, however understanding it's true power, is even more important. In this section, you will discover the money lessons you need to learn like:

- How interest can work for you or against you, and why you want it on your side.

- How credit works.

- How to balance your check book.

- How to survive on a budget.

Money doesn't have to be a mystery. In fact, it shouldn't be. What money should be is manageable. This section will help you learn how to make money in college, how to save money in college, and even how to double it!

1

FIVE MONEY LESSONS MAMMA DIDN'T KNOW

Lesson 1: Money Does Matter

Money does matter. Money matters because it is the main ingredient necessary to craft a successful financial future. Just as a carpenter needs a hammer, or a plumber needs a plunger, individuals need to use money as a tool to build their lives. It's not exactly a news flash, but it was necessary for me to understand this and it's necessary that I share it now.

Most of our lives we are sent mixed messages about money.

Everywhere you turn, you see the value put on money and the messages are saying, "Money will make you happy," "Money means choices," "CREAM-Cash rules everything around me," and "You've gotta get paid." So, what's the deal? At a time when you and most of your friends are broke, you are being bombarded with antagonistic messages like, "If you're broke, you're a joke," or "With no money, who's going to take you seriously?"

On the flip side, we are told that it doesn't matter. Pleeeeze. For people trying to convince you that money doesn't matter, it is more a matter of fiction than fact. This response is often the defense of those who are fully aware of how much it does matter.

The truth is, the only true value money has is the value we place on it. Money has intrinsic value, determined by many factors, such as our perceptions, our beliefs, inflation, and recession. It's a fine line between perception and truth. What matters even more than money is what it can do for you *if* you understand its true power, and what it can do to you if you do not.

Lesson 2: The Power of Do vs. Tell

"Do as I say and not as I do." I heard it all the time. But what neither I nor the person saying it realized is that this goes against human nature, and we often end up making the same mistakes as the people around us.

As a child, we didn't have a lot of money. Money was rarely discussed, and when it was, it seemed as if someone was always "short," "broke," "had too much month at the end of the money," or made some equally negative comment about it. Unknowingly, I developed a negative money attitude.

I was always told to "save a little," but I never saw the practice carried out. I was cautioned against "allowing money to burn a hole in my pocket," but every time someone around me got money — it was spent. Having money was a reason to celebrate because who knew when it would come around again?

It took me a long time — well after college — to realize that many of my money habits came from following the examples that I saw, rather than doing what I was told. It takes a conscious effort to change your behavior because you are often unaware that the behavior you're exhibiting is flawed.

So, here are your options: either listen to what your parents were actually saying or find a mentor who is willing to guide you through the process of walking the talk. Start saving now!

Lesson 3: How To Make a Dollar Out Of 15 Cents AND Always Pay Yourself First

Learning the importance of saving a little of everything you get is a powerful practice. Unfortunately, many people realize this too late. One of the advantages of being young is that you have time. The span between your 18th and 30th birthday could mean hundreds of thousands of earned interest dollars in your pocket. Time is a precious commodity that can't be bought, sold, or given away, and it's on your side.

The name of the game is compound interest. There are many complicated definitions for compound interest. However, a simple way of looking at compound interest would be to think of planting an acorn in the back yard when you are five. Time passes and you grow up, move away from home and return for a visit only to be surprised that the little acorn you planted and forgot about turned into a giant oak tree!

Here's the secret to compound interest: It's not how much you have, but how soon you start saving (even a little) and the longer you commit to leaving the money alone. The longer it's there, the longer it has to work for you and the bigger it will grow.

The **time value of money** says; a dollar earned and saved today will be worth more tomorrow than a dollar earned and saved in the future. This is what is called a positive rate of return on your investments.

If I've confused you, allow me to explain to you what I mean:

Consider two investors who are the same age, with the same annual income, and with similar investment goals. The only difference is that one starts investing earlier than the other.

Example: Investor 1 begins at age 25, contributes $2,000 each year for 10 years, and then stops adding money to the account.

Investor 2 begins investing at age 35 and invests $2,000 each year for 30 years.

Assuming both earn a rate of return of 8% per year after expenses, can you predict who will have the most money at 65?

Investment Summary				
Investor	Years Invested	Total Invested	Worth of Investment at Age 65	Earnings
1 — Age 25	10	$20,000	$314,870	$294,870
2 — Age 35	30	$60,000	$244,692	$184,632

Source: vanguard.com

Investor 2 is worth 22% less than Investor 1. How is this possible?

Time is the main ingredient. The compound interest had longer to work for Investor 1. Just think if Investor 1 continued to save $2,000 per year. The total amount he would have accumulated with interest compounding would be $559,562 or $314,870 more than Investor 2 accumulated!

Does the math seem wrong? Not at all — time has the ability to make a dollar out of 15 cents, if you understand the power of compounding.

If you're still confused, allow me to show you what I mean.

YOUR MONEY THROUGH THE AGES
SAVINGS GROWTH CHART

Your Age	Monthly Investment	Total Invested through age 65	Assumed rate of return			
			4%	6%	8%	10%
25	50	$24,000	$59,295	$100,072	$175,714	$318,839
30	50	$21,000	$45,839	$71,592	$115,459	$191,414

Look at the difference just five years makes!

Ok, now what? You're under 25, you're already blowing $50 a month on CD's, clothes, beer, whatever. You have it, why not save it or at least some of it. Can you see how saving can be a very good thing?

Imagine what the numbers would be if you started saving at age 19, 22, or 24. Even if you have to stop saving for a while, like Investor 1, you'll be way ahead of the people who never started. Don't wait until you're "gettin' paid" to start. There is no such thing as catch-up. Time is the best thing you've got going! Youth is a wonderful thing; use it wisely.

There are several practical reasons for you to put the principal of "Always pay yourself first" into practice. However, as you continue to read this book, you will see, or at least it's my hope, the best reason of all to pay yourself first: You might not always be able to count on family and friends to come through for you in a jam. You need to be prepared to count on YOU in cases of emergency and hardship. To be financially independent you'll need to be financially responsible.

Lesson 4: What the Poor and Middle Class Buy on Payday

"Keeping up with the Jones,'" will keep you and the Jones' in an endless cycle of debt. The truth is if you buy the hype, you'll pay for it over a lifetime.

According to the best selling book "The Millionaire Next Door" here's the real deal on wealth building. Believe it or not, most of the ice wearing, Benz drivin,' highballers ain't rich:

> *"Being frugal is the cornerstone of wealth-building. Yet far too often big spenders are promoted and sensationalized by the popular press. We are constantly barraged with media hype about so-called millionaire athletes, for example.*
>
> *"Yes, some of the members of this small population are millionaires. But if a highly skilled ball player makes $5 million a year, having $1 million in net worth is no big deal. According to our wealth equation, a $5 million earner who is thirty years of age should be worth $15 million or more. How many . . . have a level of wealth in this range? We believe only a tiny fraction. Why? Because most have a lavish lifestyle — and they can only support such a lifestyle as long as they are earning a very high income.*
>
> *But the lavish lifestyle sells TV time and newspapers. All too often young people (we) are indoctrinated with the belief that 'those who have money spend lavishly' and 'if you don't show it, you don't have it.' . . . most people who build wealth in America are hard working, thrifty, and not at all glamorous. Wealth is rarely gained through the lottery, with a home run, or in quiz show fashion."*

Still not convinced? Ask yourself this. Whatever happened to multi-platinum recording artist Kris Kross? Or what about Vanilla Ice? And you can't forget about TLC.

Many other entertainers have filed for bankruptcy. In an industry known for tough contracts on young artists, most of whom never really make it big even at their height of popularity, never receive royalty payments of more than 10 or 12 percent.

Lavish lifestyles that outpaced their income was the reason MC Hammer, Gary Coleman, Redd Foxx, Kim Bassinger, Toni Braxton, and Sherman Hemsley (yep, George "Movin' on Up" Jefferson) filed for bankruptcy. The casualties outnumber the ones who made it and kept it.

Lesson 5: Credit Isn't Evil

Upon graduating from college, and after having amassed outrageous debt, I quickly experienced the power that credit has in the world. I learned that credit isn't evil. In fact, it's necessary. If you want to know how necessary it is, just try renting a car or booking a hotel without it. And don't even attempt to get an apartment much less a video from the video store without credit.

It's difficult to explain to adults that vague advice and time honored clichés like, "Money doesn't grow on trees," "Don't let your money burn a whole in your pocket," or "A penny saved is a penny earned," are not sufficient when discussing the important things in life like money.

> *Money does matter. It's your perception of this truth that will make or break you.*

Much of the advice I got about money and credit was scant at best, and through trial and error, I found out some of the advice wasn't wholly accurate. As a young adult, human nature tells you that you know more than the adults around you and even if you mess up

50% of the time, you've gotta be doing a better job than they did. Right? Not necessarily true.

Now that I'm a little older, what I have learned is this: Money does matter. It's your perception of this truth that will make or break you. Credit isn't evil, but it can be dangerous if used without proper and specific instruction.

2

HOW BAD CREDIT CAN KILL YOUR CAREER

The Dangers of Debt

My understanding of credit was limited when I entered college. I was told to stay away from it. That was my formal introduction to credit.

I grew up in a small town and a large family. Money was always an issue. It seemed whenever I had it a portion always needed to be "contributed to the household." I couldn't wait for a time when I was on my own and all my money belonged to me.

Shortly after I'd been on campus, I began to notice that most of the people I went to school with had a credit card. Some students got cards from their parents to purchase books and school related items, others had them because they had part-time jobs. Regardless of how they got them, it seemed like those who had them had a level of sophistication that I wanted.

I had no idea how to get a credit card. I didn't even know I had the option to get one, since I didn't have a "real" job. The only thing I knew was where to apply for one. Each day as I walked to class, people frequently stopped and asked me if I wanted to apply for a credit card. They would offer all sorts of stuff to sweeten the deal if I would just stop and complete an application.

Most of the time I would keep walking, but on the day I stopped to sign on the dotted line, I had no idea that the credit card application I filled out would actually result in a credit card that would ultimately provide me with a $1,500 credit limit. I lied on the application just to get a walk-man. The representative at the table told me it was "harmless" and that they would "probably reject me anyway."

When I got the card, six weeks later, I'd forgotten that I filled out the application in the first place.

It was a nice feeling, to have a piece of plastic with my name on it and a starting credit limit of $500 attached.

I was excited and nervous at the same time. I couldn't believe that *I* had a credit card. I was an adult; a sophisticated, credit card carrying adult.

However, reality and guilt quickly ensued. What if they made a mistake? What if they found out that all the information on the application wasn't entirely true? Would I be arrested? Could I go to jail?

As I sat in my room with a flood of emotions, I vowed only

> *It was a nice feeling, to have a piece of plastic with my name on it . . .*

to use the card if it was an emergency — only if I really, truly needed it. I activated the card. My first purchase (an absolute necessity, I told myself) was a new wallet. After all, if I was going to be a credit card owner I needed a place to put it, right?

It didn't take long after I activated the card for an "emergency" to come along. It was a long weekend and everyone was leaving campus and so was I, or so I thought. My boyfriend was on his way to get me, but he was having car trouble. So, I charged a bus ticket to see him for the weekend. I mean I couldn't stay on campus, could I? I must admit it felt pretty good pulling out my credit card and signing my name on the receipt. I was smiling from ear to ear. I kept thinking this is why I needed a credit card.

To celebrate my new independence, I followed the purchase of the bus ticket with dinner and a new outfit. The whole trip cost me about $256. When I got back, I calculated my paycheck and figured it would take about two months to pay it off. It seemed very possible to manage, and since this was my emergency money, I wanted to make sure I repaid it quickly.

After a few months, I received a letter saying that I was a valued customer and because my payment history was good, I would be receiving a $300 increase! My careful financial planning was paying off — use it a little, but pay it off.

To celebrate my newfound wealth I went to the mall.

My friends were always telling me I was too uptight about using my credit card. So, I decided it was time to loosen up, have some fun. This is what I'd been waiting for, my own money to spend just as I wanted.

This newfound money was great. I was flying high! Soon I was on a roll. However, it didn't stop there.

I got a cool T-shirt when I filled out another application that got me a credit card with $1,000 credit limit. And then, there was the card I was "pre-approved" for with a $700 credit limit.

I continued to pay my original credit card payment, and I continued to be "rewarded" for my good payment habits. My credit limit went from $500 to $1,500 in no time! All of my cards were rewarding me for using them. What could be better?

Then, there were the department store cards that I applied for just to get that "additional 20% off your purchase."

Clothes, jewelry, increased credit limits, Spring Break, dinners out, gifts for friends, tough classes, increased hours at work, shoes, handbags; I was living the life I always wanted. Or, so I thought . . .

I was a good student. In fact, I was such a good student that I figured out how to complete my course requirements a full semester early just to get a jumpstart on my career in communications. In the fall of 1994, I completed my Bachelor of Science requirements and began applying and interviewing for jobs in New York City. However, there was one in particular I had my eye on. If I got this job, all would be right in my world. A job at this company would be big, bigger than big — it would be HUGE!

I thought my prayers were answered when I was called back for a second, third, and finally, a fourth interview by the company that I most wanted to work for — more than anything. I walked into the offices for my fourth interview. I was sure of myself; I knew I had the job. I was beaming. I was on top of the world.

What happened next changed my life.

As I sat as still as I could in my chair across from a woman that I admired and wanted to be like. I was stunned to silence and tears by these words, "Sanyika, I like you. In fact, everyone here likes you. You're the best candidate we've interviewed for this position. I'd love to offer you this job, I really would. However, the Junior Account Executive position that you've interviewed for comes with an expense account and a corporate credit card. In considering you for the position, we had to review your credit report. I shouldn't be telling you this, but I wanted you to know; you have a big problem. Upon further review of your credit report, we realize that you haven't been responsible with managing your personal finances. As a result, we cannot in good faith assume you will be responsible in handling ours. I'm sorry, I really am. I wish I could make an exception, but it's out of my control."

If she said anything after that, I didn't hear it. I was numb. I was devastated. I was screwed.

Before I graduated from college, I had racked up $15,000 in unsecured debt (more than ½ from credit cards). I had managed to be approved for nine credit cards in three years, with no real income!

Soon, it became very hard to keep up with all my minimum payments and still have a life. I knew that I hadn't paid a couple of my credit card bills on time, but it wasn't my fault (or so I thought). No matter how much I sent them, it was never enough. They were always calling me, sending me reminders that my account was past due. I knew it was past due and I was doing everything I could to keep up. I even got a cash advance from one card to pay the balance on another, but they were taking my whole paycheck!

With the burden of my course load there was no way I could have worked more hours. Besides, it wasn't such a big deal. They'd get their money, eventually. I had a plan. "When I get my high paying job in New York City, I'll pay them off," I thought.

My plan wasn't working. It wasn't supposed to happen this way. I was scared.

I cursed the credit card companies for giving me the cards. I blamed my parents. I blamed everyone and everything, but myself. I immediately looked for the easiest and fastest way to get out of the trouble I was in.

I fulfilled my dream of moving to New York, but it was far from a dream, it was more like a nightmare. I was very eager to prove my independence. Funny that I

> *I blamed my parents. I blamed everyone and everything, but myself.*

never reached the independence that I longed for, because I became a slave to my creditors.

I got a job. Most people would have loved to have it. But it wasn't what I wanted, and worst of all, it wasn't in my major! I felt like a failure. I was miserable. I lived in one of the most exciting cities in the world and could not enjoy it.

Imagine my frustration as I watched my new friends and co-workers go to cool restaurants and hip nightclubs that I could not afford. In fact, I could hardly afford the rent and food at the same time. After college I swore I would never eat macaroni and cheese as a meal again. I wasn't able to keep that promise to myself. There were many peanut butter and jelly days ahead.

I was 22, with an entry-level job and $500 worth of *minimum* payments on my cards each month, not to mention any other expenses to be considered. I was frustrated and scared. My job did not offer overtime pay, even though I regularly worked 10-hour days. And getting a part-time job wasn't an option. I had nowhere to turn. I felt lost and desperate.

My first attempt at financial relief was to respond to a small classified ad that promised to "wipe my credit report clean." I desperately wanted this to be true so I could move out of my apartment and get a better job. (Having roommates in college was one thing, but now I was an adult.) I had been late with several of my payments and knew that it would hurt my chances of securing a lease on my own.

It seemed like it was worth a shot, so I scraped up the $250 and sent a money order to a PO Box. After several long weeks of waiting and no change to my credit report, I received a photocopied "ransom type" letter. It coldly apologized that they could not help me, and the $250 fee was non-refundable because they "tried to contact the credit reporting agencies on my behalf with no response."

My second attempt came a few months later when I responded to a radio ad that claimed they would help me manage my debt load. All I had to do was "pay one low monthly payment," and they would "do the rest." This was music to my ears! One payment and all my bills could be paid, *and* I'd still have money left over?

I quickly called the toll free number and listened to the pre-recorded message that prompted me to leave my name and contact information for someone to return my call. Two days later I received a call back from a "case counselor" that asked lots of questions about my payment history and involvement with any other "services like this one." Within a week, I had completed the application and sent all of my personal information along with the requested $199 money order for processing.

By the end of the month, I had received a "summary of savings" statement outlining the "terms of agreement." I agreed to pay a $300 monthly payment, as well as, a $75 "handling fee" each month. I wasn't happy with the arrangement, but it was (at least I thought) better than I was doing on my own.

After four months with the service everything seemed to be going fine. I mailed my money order by the fifth of each month and, in turn, my payments were sent to each of my creditors on my behalf (or at least I thought so).

In the original agreement, I was told **not** to contact my creditors (that was fine with me) because "it could delay or adversely affect the negotiation process." I would find out the true reason soon enough.

I first became suspicious when the creditors, which had stopped calling, started to call again. My fears were confirmed when I received a cancellation letter (for one of my last active cards — eight had already been "closed by credit grantor") in the mail due to non-payment.

When I tried to contact my debt management case counselor I was greeted by a telephone operator recording that informed me in a monotone voice, "the number you have dialed has been disconnected. There is no additional information about this number. If you feel you've reached the number in error, please hang up and try your call again." So, after hitting redial at least 10 times, and then actually redialing several more times by pressing one number at a time very slowly to be sure, I sat stunned and felt defeated.

I considered filing bankruptcy, but I thought better of it. I heard some horror stories about bankruptcy and I wasn't about to find out if they were true — besides I couldn't come up with the $399 processing   fee!

Sadly,   I   was   not   alone   .   .   .

According to the American Bankruptcy Institute, "Personal bankruptcy filings for the 12 months ended March 31, 1996 accounted for 94.7 percent of the total bankruptcy filings, and increased by 17.8 percent over the 12-month period ended March 31, 1995. This increase comes in the wake of a steady increase in consumer debt, which has expanded briskly for the past two years. Credit card delinquencies are at a ten-year high, and monthly debt service stands at 17 percent of total household income."

This is not to be taken lightly. Currently, personal bankruptcy is a growing problem for adults under 25 as they come face to face with their enormous debt load. Bankruptcy is not the answer. If you think your credit is bad now, try walking

> *Credit card delinquencies are at a ten-year high.*

around for 7–10 years with a bankruptcy rope around your neck. The consequences are inconceivable.

Finally, but not before countless sleepless nights, and many threatening phone calls from collection agency representatives, I realized that if something was going to change, then it was up to me.

I started by being honest with myself. It was not easy . . . being personally responsible rarely is. Then I started looking for every book, magazine, and source for factual and proven information that I could use to get me on track.

My quest presented me with several choices for information. The problem was that there didn't seem to be one that had all of the information that I needed. Many books were either very hard to understand or didn't apply to my situation.

This was very frustrating but I pressed on anyway. I decided that if I took bits and pieces of information from several sources, it would be better than just being frustrated by the fact that it wasn't all neatly found in one place.

The process began. It was hard. It was necessary. It was worth it. I promised myself that if I ever got out of the mess I was in, I would do everything I could to help others avoid it all together, or at least, have the benefit of the information and techniques I used all in one place. From this promise, I began my new career in debt education, as well as this book and the Crack 'Da Code campus tour.

My purpose in writing this book is to reveal the information you need to survive as you transition into the world of financial independence. Understanding the way the world works will allow you to navigate safely the landmines it inevitably places in your path.

———— ►⸗⸗◄⸗⸗◄ ————

3

THE BASICS OF BANKING

Most young adults obtain their first checking account in college. Many banks have local branches near the colleges or even on the campus of the university you attend.

Here are four things to consider when choosing a bank:

1. **Ease of use** — Will parents or relatives be able to deposit or transfer funds when you need them to with relative ease. You will also want to know how convenient it will be to make a deposit, check your balance, or even bank on-line.

2. **Monthly service charges and fees** — Every dime counts at this phase of your financial life. Be sure you are not paying for fees that another bank may waive or not charge at all. Be aware of fees charged for ATM use, checks processed, and going below the minimum balance required.

3. **Location and number of branches—** It's important to take the long view here. Will you be able to visit your bank during your breaks from school? Will there be a branch in the area you plan to move after college? What are the banking hours? Do they have a "late night" which will allow you to conduct business with a live teller after 4:00 P.M.?

4. **What services are available to you as a bank customer?** —Is automatic bill payment an option? Will cancelled checks be returned with your statements? Will your accounts be linked?

Debit vs. Credit Cards

For many college students the appeal of opening a checking account is in getting a Visa® or MasterCard® logo debit card, sometimes called a check card. The cool thing about these cards is their ability to be used interchangeably as a debit or a credit card. Unfortunately, what makes them cool also makes them confusing.

Debit cards with credit card logos are debit cards. By design, a debit card is attached to your checking account and allows you to electronically withdraw funds from the account. In order for the transaction to be approved, you must have the funds available in your checking account. Using this card, regardless of the logo's presence, will not help you establish credit (I'll discuss establishing credit in detail in chapter 4) and the card is only operable when funds are available.

Debit cards are incredibly convenient and speed transactions that were once handled by checks. When accepting a debit card from your bank, be sure you know what fees and rules apply to its use.

Credit Unions

I am a big fan of credit unions because of their personal service and low fees. However, they aren't for everyone.

For the most part, CUs (credit unions) tend to charge lower rates on loans and offer higher rates of interest on savings accounts. In addition, approximately two-thirds offer free checking with low or no minimum balance requirement. Fees for services such as bounced checks, cashiers checks, and ATM use also tend to be lower than most banks.

That said there are a few things about credit unions that might make them less than attractive to the average bank customer.

1. Most CUs don't have their own ATMs. And, although they issue debit cards that will work in standard ATM machines, you might be charged a fee by the bank that owns the ATM.

2. Very few CUs have multiple branch locations — they tend to be in a central area with one major branch. Therefore, transactions are often conducted by mail or electronically. This is not always an option for students requiring immediate assistance and access.

3. Most CUs require you to be a member of an organization or association in order to be a member of the CU (i.e. Firefighters Credit Union, Desert Schools Credit Union). You might be eligible for membership if you are a family member or friend of someone who already belongs to the CU and they agree to sponsor you.

To find out more about credit unions call (800) 358-5710 and ask for the phone number to the credit union league in your area.

Balancing Your Checkbook

Opening a checking account is just the beginning. There are realities of having a checking account that you need to be aware of.

The first thing you need to do is balance your checkbook. This fundamental step will take discipline. However, it will ensure you always know how much money you have, or don't have, to operate with.

Step 1: Enter each check you write into your check ledger; include date, description/reason for purchase, check number, and amount of check.

Step 2: Deduct the amount paid from the account balance. Always carry the balance from one entry to the next to ensure accurate accounting.

Step 3: Enter each deposit/credit and add it to the account balance (include the date and the description).

Step 4: Note all ATM transactions and any fees from the ATM used or that your bank might impose. (This is core to balancing your account.)

Step 5: Add any direct deposits and be sure to note when the funds will be available.

Step 6: Deduct monthly bank fees and service charges from your account.

Step 7: Compare your monthly statements from the bank with your check ledger. This will ensure that you haven't been overcharged and that you are fully aware of your account activity.

We've all been in a financial jam before. However, you don't want to take a bounced check lightly. Each banking institution has specific rules and regulations as it pertains to bounced checks, however, they all plug into one system for their information about customers with a history of bad banking practices: ChexSystems. This agency is to the banking industry what credit-reporting agencies are to the credit card lenders.

ChexSystems tracks your banking practices and reports that information to lending institutions when you attempt to open a new bank account, write a check, or make a transaction that requires a banking institution. Having negative information on your record with this agency could keep you out of the banking game for up to five years. The main violations reported are:

- A history of account mishandling.

- Outstanding debt.

ChexSystems also collects information on savings accounts as well. Both banks and credit unions rely on the information provided to make account related decisions.

To learn more about ChexSystems, or to order a copy of your ChexSystems Consumer report, visit www.chexhelp.com or call 1 (800) 428-9623.

When opening your checking account sign up for **overdraft protection** or bounced-check payment if possible. This is a pre-approved loan that goes into action whenever a check is posted against an account with insufficient funds. You will be required to pay the funds back and usually there is a fee, as well as interest, associated with this option.

This is a safety net, *not* additional money. Used correctly, it could save you the expense and embarrassment of a bounced check. Used incorrectly, you will incur a high interest bill.

Another service you might look into is the electronic bill payment service. This service is an awesome way to keep track of your expenses, ensure your bills are paid on time, and avoid fees you might otherwise incur for writing multiple checks.

Getting to know the branch manager of your bank could be a lifesaver. When you open your account, be sure to introduce yourself to the branch manager and say hello whenever you're in the bank. Make sure they at least know your face. This could go a long way if you ever get into a unique situation, or get charged a fee for which there was an extenuating circumstance. Have a name relationship with the person who could waive a fee or erase a charge.

> *Introduce yourself to the branch manager and say hello whenever you're in the bank. Make sure they at least know your face.*

My final point about banking is one that we often take too lightly. ATM use. Do not attempt to manage your checking account via the ATM. One of the most common reasons student's accounts are overdrawn is due to ATM overuse and associated fees. You could easily bounce a check, if you are relying on the information provided solely by the ATM.

For example, if you have a balance of $150 in your checking account and write a check for $50 at the grocery store, it could take up to seven days for the funds to be withdrawn from your checking account. What would happen if, two days after you wrote the check at the grocery store, you took out $60 at an ATM for the weekend (with a fee of $2.50), and a few days later, you realized you needed another $20? If you made no record of the earlier check transactions, you see how easily your account could get out of control.

Again, **do not** use the ATM to manage your checking account. Balance it with your check ledger

(you can find more information on tracking your expenses in chapter 6)

According to The National Banking Association, banking customers paid more than $2.56 billion dollars in ATM fees in 2002. That number is staggering! Be sure that you are keeping a close watch on your ATM use and the fees associated with that use.

How to Read Your Monthly Bank Statement

You'll want to get in the habit of checking your monthly bank statement. This will help keep track of your spending as well as become a good habit that will help you manage your finances more responsibly.

When reading your statements, here's what to look for:

- Compare checks written to checks paid to see if you have outstanding checks that need to be covered before assuming that you have additional money.

- Check to see if the full amount of deposits made were posted (many banks will place a "funds hold" on checks not drawn from their own accounts).

- Understand the ATM service charges and monthly fees. Don't be surprised by these deductions; know the costs up front.

- What interest, if any, can you earn? If you have maintained a set balance during the defined cycle, you could be paid interest.

- Do they have a toll-free number or customer service hotline for answers to questions 24 hours, seven days a week?

Having a checking and savings account is a step in the right direction to being financially responsible.

These accounts are valuable in helping you understand money matters.

4

UNDERSTANDING YOUR CREDIT

Understanding Credit: Credit 101

You've heard that ignorance is bliss. Not so with finances. Moreover, just because you "didn't know better," doesn't mean the consequences are any less painful.

I hope you're reading this before you need it. If not, and you're inclined to blame your creditors, your parents, or your dog for your problems — go ahead; it might even make you feel better for a moment. However, when your pity party is over you'll need to be ready to take responsibility and do something about your situation. Here's how: Education and knowledge is truly powerful.

Credit Cards vs. Charge Cards

I had no idea that there was a difference between a credit card and a charge card. In fact, there are three categories of cards available:

The easiest way to explain the difference between a credit card and a charge card is to highlight their most obvious difference.

A credit card allows you to charge purchases against a predetermined credit limit and affords you the option to pay the balance in full without penalty, or you have the option to pay only a portion of the balance as long as the amount due is less than your credit limit. Carrying over a balance from month to month is essentially the way you establish a credit history. Each month your payment tendencies are reported to the credit reporting agencies. Traditional credit cards are: MasterCard® and VISA®

A charge card allows you to charge purchases, however, you are required to pay the balance in full at the end of each billing cycle. Again, your payment tendencies are reported to the credit reporting agencies. Examples of charge cards are: American Express® and Diners Club®

- **Bankcards** issued by banks. This includes Visa, MasterCard, and Discover Card. These credit cards allow you to carry a balance from month to month, as long as you stay within the pre-determined credit limit.

- **Travel and entertainment** charge cards, such as American Express and Diners Club that require payment in full by the end of the billing cycle.

- **Store credit cards** are good only in the issuing stores. Sears is the largest issuer of these types of cards. Oil/gas companies, phone companies, and local and national department stores follow them. Most of these cards allow you to carry a balance from month to month, as long as you stay within the pre-determined charge limit.

Terms & Definitions

Here are some important terms you might come across in credit card brochures, applications, or discussions with potential lenders:

- **Annual fee** — a flat, yearly charge similar to a membership fee. Many companies offer "no annual fee" cards. Lenders who do charge them are often willing to waive the fee to keep your business, just ask.

- **Annual percentage rate (APR)** — the yearly percentage rate of the finance charge.

- **Finance charge** —the dollar amount you pay to use credit. Besides interest costs, it may include other charges, such as **cash advance fees** that are charged against your card when you borrow cash from the lender. You generally pay higher interest on cash advances than on purchases. Read the fine print.

- **Fixed rate** — a fixed annual percentage rate of the finance charge.

- **Grace period** — a time, about 25 days, during which you can pay your credit card bill without paying a finance charge (see below for more details).

- **Interest rate** — interest rates on credit card plans change over time. Some are tied to changes in other interest rates, such as the **prime rate** or the **Treasury Bill rate**. These are called **variable rate plans**. Others are not explicitly tied to changes in other interest rates and are called **fixed rate plans**.

- **Introductory rate** — a temporary, lower APR that usually lasts for about six months before converting to the normal fixed or variable rate.

- **Variable rate** — prime rate (which varies) plus an added percentage (For example, your rate may be prime rate, plus 3.9 percent).

Credit Offers and Agreements

Few consumers want to admit that they haven't read, or worse, don't understand the terms of their credit card agreements. We often find out that what we don't know can hurt us and cost us in the long run. You may be surprised to find what is hidden in the fine print of your credit card agreement.

Consumers receive countless credit card solicitations each year, many of which go unopened and ignored. Yet, when they finally stop to read them and review the fine print, it's downright scary.

Some offers are vague at best, giving little explanation of the charges you could incur. Others have ridiculous rules they expect you to follow. But, the most startling fine print rules are the limitations they use to control your spending choices.

Are you aware that your credit card company can periodically review your credit card account? This is a standard practice. Besides, it's in the agreement. How else would they know when to present all of those hard to resist offers? However, are you also aware that these same companies review your credit report to see how much debt you accumulate with their competitors and other lenders? Check the fine print, it's often in there, and it could cost you your credit card.

With some credit card companies, you could be penalized with higher interest charges, or even have your account canceled, if the company requires that you limit the total amount you charge on other credit cards. Don't blame your creditors. You agreed to it in the first place. Do yourself a favor. Never sign anything that you haven't fully read, or that you don't totally agree with. Haste really does equal waste.

Billing Cycles

Billing cycles and grace periods are also discussed in detail in the fine print. It is up to you to understand what they mean to you.

Interest rates can range from a low 4.7% to a high 25%. The average is about 14.45%. Interest works in conjunction with billing cycles, and could be quite costly if you are not aware of what is in your credit cards' agreement.

Under almost all credit card plans, the grace period only applies if you pay your balance in full each month. It does not apply if you carry a balance forward. In addition, the grace period does not apply to cash advances.

Most cards use one cycle billing that consists of as many as 30 days in a cycle or as few as 15 days. A billing cycle is the amount of time that a creditor allows to pass before calculating the amount of money spent.

For example, if you have a 30 day billing cycle, which starts on the 1st of each month and ends on the 30th, you would be required to pay a portion of the balance for purchases made within that time frame. The system usually runs a month behind itself. Your payment for purchases made in the month of June would actually be due in July.

If you have a revolving balance charge card (i.e MasterCard, Visa, Discover), you have the option of paying your balance in full without incurring a finance charge (interest). Or, the credit card company will calculate a portion of the total balance which you will be responsible for in addition to the finance charge.

It is your responsibility to be aware of your credit card company's billing practices and pay your bill in a timely manner. If you fail to comply, it could mean late fees, penalties, and additional charges, that over time, can add up and negatively affect your credit rating.

Services and Protections

There are a few other things about credit cards worth mentioning, like: "services" and "protections." These include credit card insurance, rebates, skip-a-payment offers, and shopping service offers. All are additional benefits of having a credit card, but it's another perfect opportunity to prove the fine print point. Always read what you're agreeing to. Just because it's available doesn't mean you need to have it. Let's look at some of these.

Credit Card Insurance

In my opinion, if you decide to take any credit card insurance offers, rental-car collision and travel accident insurance are the two most worthwhile insurance choices. Why pay $7 to $15 per day for the insurance a rental car company will charge, when you can use the coverage of the card on which you charged it? The collision damage waiver (CDW) usually pays the difference between the repair/replacement cost and the amount that your personal insurance company will pay.

As for the travel accident insurance. The credit card companies can afford to automatically give you $300,000 in accident insurance when you purchase your airline ticket with their credit card, because, the likelihood of air calamity is relatively low. So they look good and you feel protected.

Credit Card Protection Insurance, I've found, usually works in the issuers favor. The offer seems so practical. No one wants to find themselves in a position where they can't pay their bills, so they offer you peace of mind for a few extra dollars each month. Basically, the insurance works like this:

- There are certain restrictions on when you can use the insurance. For some companies you must be *totally** disabled or involuntarily unemployed. If you're having financial hard times unrelated to the reasons above, this insurance doesn't help.

- You must wait 30 days before claiming the benefits.

- The insurance only covers the minimum monthly payments. Meanwhile the interest is still calculated, and there may be a cap on how much of the balance they will insure.

- Prior to the claim, the account must be in good standing. If you were late or missed a couple of payments prior to attempting to claim the insurance benefits, not only will you loose money, you'll also have no insurance coverage.

- Again, understanding all of your options will make you an educated consumer. Knowledge is power.

Rebates:

Getting a 1% to 3% rebate from credit card purchases is nice, but it hardly covers the interest you pay on a credit card with a revolving balance. (A balance which is carried over from month to month.) Any money that you get back through a rebate should go right back to the credit card company to pay down your balance. It's okay to charge all of your purchases

---

* Read the Fine Print. Each company has very different definitions of what it means to be disabled. Protect yourself. Know the facts.

on a card that offers you a rebate or points, but remember that you are still obligated to pay your balance and no amount of points compares to the satisfaction of knowing your bills are paid.

Skip-A-Payment Offers

These offers are extended to valued customers. If you're in a jam it can come in handy because you have the creditor's permission to withhold payment. However be aware of what you're agreeing to here. Understand that interest is being compounded (calculated).

For example, if you have a balance of $1,782.81 at a 9.95% APR with a 30 day billing cycle with a minimum monthly payment of $103.00, and you skip a payment; you will pay less on the principle and more to the finance charge when you make your next payment.

To break it down further, of the $103 you pay each month $87.93 should go to the principle (total balance minus interest) and the remaining $15.07 should be applied to the finance charge (interest). In this case the balance would be $1,694.88.

However, when you skip-a-payment, the following month $74.64 goes to the principle and $28.36 to the finance charge. In this case, your balance is $1,708.17. You do the math; if you buy yourself a month's worth of breathing room, be sure you can really afford it.

In the following pages, you will be given tools to help you better understand how credit can play a positive role in your college experience and serve you well into the future.

Remember, it's all about education and instruction.

Beware & Watch Out

Watch out for those "check's in the mail" offers you receive with a letter of congratulations. If you didn't work for it, have a relative who sent it to you, or win the campus beauty pageant; then rip it to shreds! Some lenders send "live pre-approved checks" in the mail hoping that you'll be excited enough, or desperate enough, just to sign on the dotted line. If you do, you're making a deal with the devil. What they're hoping you won't notice (until it's too late) is that the $2,500 check they've given you has a 23.99% variable APR, and a $100 per year annual fee. And don't forget about the excessive fees that also come with the card. So, if you ever get this "special offer" to pay off your bills, fix your car, or make that special purchase, beware and watch out!

Knowing which credit card is right for you and how to read a credit card statement is important. You'll have several offers, but it will be necessary to look at each offer **very carefully**. Know what you are agreeing to in advance. Remember, "Once I sign on the line, it's mine." You can't tell a company that you didn't read their policies and procedures in advance. Ignorance is no excuse; the consequences are still the same.

Credit Card Comparison Worksheet

Using the chart on page 53, take the time to compare the credit cards you are considering applying for. Calculate the annual fee and the APR you'll be charged. How long is the grace period? What's the equation used in determining the finance charge? Will there be fees? What kind? How much? What's the maximum credit limit? What services does the company offer? Read the fine print, learn the facts, and make an educated decision.

CREDIT CARD	ANNUAL FEE	APR	GRACE PERIOD	FINANCE CHARGE CALCULATION	TRANSACTION FEE	CREDIT LIMIT	SERVICES

Source: Indiana Department of Financial Institutions

A credit card statement provides information, such as how and when you've used your credit card, how much you owe, interest rates, how much your minimum payment is, and how much credit you have left. The statement also gives you the periodic interest rate, total finance charges, the balance upon which your finance charges were computed, any fees incurred, and contact information.

How to Read Your Monthly Credit Card Statement

After reviewing the sample credit card statement on this page, answer the following questions to be sure you fully understand the information on the credit card statement.

Your First Bank		CREDIT CARD STATEMENT		SEND PAYMENT TO Box 1234 Anytown, USA54321
ACCOUNT NUMBER 4321-1234-4321	NAME JOHN DOE	STATEMENT DATE 8/26/02		PAYMENT DUE DATE 9/24/02
NEW BALANCE $125.24	CREDIT LINE $1,200.00	CREDIT AVAILABLE $1,074.76		MINIMUM PAYMENT DUE $10.00

REFERENCE	DATE SOLD	DATE POSTED	ACTIVITY SINCE LAST STATEMENT		AMOUNT
489CE75001250			PAYMENT	THANK YOU	-183.30
109 94 SCR0	8/3/02	8/19/02	RECORD RECYCLER	ANYTOWN USA	14.35
80 102052	8/4/02	8/19/02	BEEF O RAMA REST	ANYTOWN USA	50.30
7058H J092	8/1/02	8/18/02	GREAT EXPECTATIONS	BIG CITY USA	27.30
3H RF928BA	8/2/02	8/21/02	OMG-GCL PETROLEUM	ANYTOWN USA	12.38
3F90HW582	7/08/02	8/14/02	SHIRTS N SUCH	TINYVILLE USA	48.10

Previous balance	183.30	Current Amount Due	125.24
Purchases (+)	125.24	Amount Past Due	
Cash Advances (+)		Amount Over Credit Limit	
Payments (-)	183.30	Minimum Payment Due	10.00
Credits (-)			
FINANCE CHARGES (+)			
Late Charges (+)			
NEW BALANCE (=)	125.24		

FINANCE CHARGE SUMMARY	PURCHASES	ADVANCES	For Customer Service Call: 1-800-XX-XX-XXX For Lost or Stolen Card, Call: 1-800-XX-X-XXX 24-Hour Telephone Numbers
Periodic Rate	1.35%	1.85%	
ANNUAL PERCENTAGE RATE	16.20%	19.20%	

See reverse side for Billing Error Information.

Source: Indiana Department of Financial Institutions

1. What is the date of the statement?

2. What is the APR? What does APR mean?

3. What is the corresponding periodic rate?

4. What is the new balance? What is the minimum payment due?

5. What was the previous balance?

6. How many charges were made during the billing cycle?

7. How many credits and payments were made during the billing cycle?

8. Were there any charges for late payments? If so, how much?

9. What is the total amount of the credit line?

10. What is the total amount of available credit?

11. What is the total amount of charges made during the current billing period?

12. Was there a finance charge for the current billing cycle? If not, why?

13. What is the account number on the statement? When is the payment due date?

14. If you chose to pay only the minimum payment, how much would you owe on your next bill, if no additional purchases were made? How did you arrive at that answer?

15. What percentage of the total amount charged does the minimum payment represent?

ANSWERS: 1) 8/13/02; 2) 19.80%; Annual Percentage Rate; 3) 1.65%; 4) $125.24, $10.00; 5) $168.80; 6) Four; 7) One; 8) No; 9) $1200.00; 10) 1074.76; 11) $125.24; 12) No. Because the bill was paid in full from the previous month; 13) 4321–1234–4321, 9/24/02; 14) $138.06 - Current amount due minus Minimum payment due equals $115.24; $115.24 multiplied by the APR equals $22.82; $22.82 plus $115.24 equals $138.06; 15) 8%.

How to Establish Credit

Although it seems like credit is easy to get when you're in college, you might have been rejected for a credit card or any other type of account that requires you to have a "sufficient credit history established." It's the chicken and the egg dilemma. But here are some tips to help you establish a credit history and get the credit that you deserve.

- Start with a secured card. This will provide you the convenience of a credit card while establishing an on-time payment history and good credit management skills.

- Establish a mobile phone account, cable bill, or utility bill in your name. All of these options require you to provide your social security number when applying. Paying these bills on time will result in building a positive credit profile.

- Become a co-applicant on your parent or guardian's checking account or credit card. This will allow you to have an account in your name while establishing credit and good money management practices, under the supervision of someone with an established credit history.

- Prove your responsibility and stability by getting and keeping a part-time job, and/or consistently using the same address. (If you are away from home and cannot use a physical address, get an account with a mail service that accepts mail on your behalf, but stay away from post office boxes. You need an actual address.)

- If you are working at your college, you may be able to get a small loan through the campus credit union. It could be a good place for you to establish credit.

Beware, it might be tempting to take advantage of a "great opportunity" to establish credit by purchasing a car or other high priced item. But usually, first time buyers are charged a ridiculous APR, so consider first using the tips above to establish a credit history.

You can also have a parent or guardian help you with a down payment. Then you carry the remaining loan balance. When you finish paying off the small loan balance, you have established yourself as a creditworthy person and should find it easier to get credit later on, and, more importantly, at a lower interest rate.

Tips for Protecting Your Credit Rating

Once you have begun the process of establishing credit, it is necessary to protect it at all costs. Guard your credit rating fiercely, as you would your favorite outfit, your car/truck, or whatever else you hold sacred. Don't let anyone or anything that could leave a spot on it come close. Here are some do's and don'ts for protecting your credit rating:

- DO — Pay your credit card balance in full, or at least, pay the minimum payment *and* the finance charges.

- DO — Mail your bills in with sufficient time for "snail mail" to reach its destination. A good rule is to put the check in the mail at least seven days before the due date. Or, even better, commit to paying your bills online. You'll still need to pay the bill at least three days before the due date to allow for processing.

- DON'T — Use your card for cash advances.

- DON'T — Pay the bill with your credit card when having dinner with friends, and then collect the cash from them. It's too tempting to use the cash for something else. Once you start the habit it will be hard to break, and you'll be over your limit in no time.

- DO — Leave plenty of room on your credit card for real emergencies. You will be charged over the limit fees if you spend more than you have available, and that looks bad on your credit report.

- DON'T — Spend up to the maximum credit limit. This is a tempting way to apply for more credit before paying down what you've spent.

- DO — Call your credit card company and ask questions about what's on your statement. If in doubt, find out. Ignorance is no excuse; and there are often deadlines imposed for contesting charges against your account.

- DON'T — Co-sign for a friend or relative, unless you can prove they can pay. Now really think about this. If they can prove their creditworthiness to the bank, they wouldn't need you to co-sign for them. By co-signing, you're telling the lender that you will be responsible for the debt load. It could wreck your relationship and ruin your credit.

- DO — Request, at least twice a year, a copy of your credit report and know what it says about you. Here's what should *not* be on your file:

  ❖ Information about race, color, or religion.

  ❖ Criminal charges not resulting in conviction.

  ❖ Criminal charges older than seven years.

- ❖ Credit information older than seven years (except bankruptcy).
- ❖ Health or healthcare information.

Here is a guideline on what your rating means:

NUMBER	RATING
R0	Too new to rate; approved but not used.
R1	Pays within 30 days of billing, or pays as agreed.
R2	Pays in more than 30 days, but less than 60, or one payment past due.
R3	Pays in more than 60 days, but less than 90, or two payments past due.
R4	Pays in more than 90 days, but less than 120, or three or more payments past due.
R5	Account is at least 120 days past due, but is not yet rated R9.
R6	No rating exists.
R7	Paid through a consolidation order, consumer proposal, or credit counseling debt management program.
R8	Repossession.
R9	Bad debt or placed for collection or bankruptcy.

Source: CBC News

The final thing about protecting your credit rating is understanding what credit ratings and credit scores mean to you. A **credit score** is a "grade," so to speak, assigned to you by the credit bureaus when they print your credit report. Basically, it's a calculation, which considers length of credit history, number of open accounts, outstanding loans, and public record information. The Beacon FICO score is what most lenders use in rating your credit worthiness.

Your credit score is the single most important factor in determining whether you'll get approved for a car loan, a refinance loan, or credit cards, and what your APR will be. If your score is low, you'll pay very high interest rates. A better score means more options and lower rates. Here are things that can affect your score:

- How much you are paying on your accounts.
- How much you currently owe.
- How long your accounts have been open.
- What types of credit you use (secured, unsecured, student loans).
- How much credit you use compared to the amount available to you.
- How often and how recently you have applied for credit.

What Bad Credit Means to You

I've said several times that "ignorance is no excuse." Unfortunately, I had to learn that the hard way. If you read my story in chapter two, you know about the difficult time I had paying my bills and getting a job. Maybe you read it and thought, "that won't happen to me," or "I know how to use credit responsibly."

In the event that my story was vague, you couldn't relate, or it didn't apply to you. I want to be very specific about what bad credit will mean to you in the future:

- Getting a mortgage will be difficult. Getting a mortgage with a low or manageable APR will be impossible.

- You could be declined for a checking account, or denied the privilege of opening other types of accounts with a bank.

- You will be denied jobs that require credit checks and corporate expense accounts.

- You will be denied for additional credit cards or for credit cards with low APRs.

- Your apartment application will be denied.

- You cannot buy furniture, computers, or anything on credit.

- All potential creditors will classify you as a high risk, and you'll be charged the highest possible interest rate.

5

IMPROVING YOUR CREDIT

If you are looking to change your current credit status, you now have a better understanding about credit cards and are ready to make educated credit decisions in the future. Here are some options you need, and deserve, to know for improving your credit status and reducing debt. Again, education is the main ingredient.

Request a Copy of Your Credit Report

First, you must request a copy of your credit report. There are three major credit reporting agencies (CRAs). Sometimes called "The Big Three (TB3)." They gather, store, and distribute information about you, your credit, and your payment history.

- **Equifax**
  Equifax Credit Information Services, Inc.
  P.O. Box 740241
  Atlanta, GA 30374
  (800) 685-1111

- **Experian**
  P.O. Box 2002
  Allen, TX 75013
  (888) 397-3742

- **Trans Union, LLC Consumer Disclosure Center**
  P.O. Box 1000
  Chester, PA 19022
  (800) 888-4213

Generally, requesting a copy of your credit report is a simple process. To get a copy of your report: you should contact all of the three major CRAs via mail, telephone, or the Internet. If you're requesting a copy for the first time it will be necessary to put the request in writing. A copy of your report can be obtained for approximately $8.00 each.

A free copy of your credit report can be obtained if you have been denied credit within 30 to 60 days. In addition, you can receive a free copy of your report even if you do not meet the above requirements. The Fair Credit Reporting Act (FCRA) requires that free reports be provided to persons who are unemployed and job hunting, people on welfare, and people who believe their credit file is inaccurate or erroneous due to credit fraud.

Although $8.00 is the standard cost per copy, some states have unique regulations or charge different fees. Refer to the chart below for the requirements of your state:

STATE	FEE per copy
Connecticut	$5.00
Maine	$3.00
Maryland	Call (800) 233-7654
Colorado, Georgia, Massachusetts, and Vermont	Call (800) 548-4548
All other states	$8.00

If you've never run your credit report before, you should get the Three-in-One Merged Credit Report, which is a big credit report made up of three single credit reports from the TB3: Equifax, Experian, and Trans Union.

This report is a good idea since each credit bureau reports different types of information. One credit bureau could have accurate information in your credit file, while the other two have errors that could keep you from getting approved for any type of credit.

Whether you get a Three-in-One Merged Credit Report, or three individual credit reports, the choice is yours. The important thing is to take action and find out what your credit report is saying about you.

The request process takes approximately 7-10 business days. To protect your privacy and to ensure your identity, it is necessary to include the following information with your written request.

- Your full name, including middle initial and generation (e.g. Sr., Jr., II or III).

- Current mailing address, including zip code.

- Previous address, if your address has changed within the last five years.

- Social Security number.

- Date and year of birth.

- Photocopy of a document that verifies your identity and address where the credit report should be mailed to (e.g. utility bill or driver's license).

Reviewing Your Credit Report

There are several methods in which credit information is collected, which include:

- **Manual forms** — Copies of your credit application are sent to CRAs to verify your information.

- **Instant information update links** — Data banks are linked to share information.

- **Phone inquiry** — When a lender calls a CRA (or vice versa) to verify information in your file, the information is shared, updated, or added.

- **Public records** — such as Birth and Marriage or Death certificates are public information, and can be obtained from courthouses and federal bureaus. CRAs also retain information on divorce, judgments, property liens, foreclosures, and bankruptcy. This information is easily accessible and available to the public.

You must carefully review your report for erroneous information (i.e. incorrect spelling of name, outdated account information, etc.). It is up to you to police your credit report and ensure that the information contained is correct, accurate, and up-to-date.

Here is what a typical credit report looks like:

REPORT DATE: 04/30/00		Reference Number:		0-00-000-00-000-000		
		Membership Number:		5555-5555		
NAME(S): SMITH, RICHARD D.		Social Security Nbr:	111-22-3333		AGE: 34	

CURR ADDRESS: 2956 101 ST STREET, CHICAGO, IL 60519

REPORT SUMMARY:

Oldest Account	8/83	Real Estate Bal	$94,000	Current Accts	21	Public		Collection
Credit Accounts	21	Installment Bal	$9,062	Revolving Credit Avail	98%	Records		Accounts
Closed Accounts	0	Revolving Bal	$1,204	Was Delq/Derog	0	EFX 0		EFX 0
Inquiries	7	Total R/E Pmt	$922	Now Delq/Derog	0	XPN 0		XPN 0
Import max	4	Total Other Pmt	$43	Past Due Amt	$0	TUC 0		TUC 0

Account Name/Number/Type of Account

Credit Bureau (DC)	Date Opened	Date Open	High/Limit	Mthly Pymt	Account Balance	Last Rptd	Account Status	Past Due Amt	Last Dclnq	Past Due 30 60 90+	Hist Date	Historical Acct Status

AMERICAN EXPRESS C000150000017 90 DAY ACCOUNT
(01) XPN I 10-87 2400 N/A 578 12-91 DEL 90   01 00 01 07-91 2 111111 111111110 111 111

CIT BANK VISA570033674 REVOLVING
(01) XPN I 10-85 500 20 108 10-01 DEL 60   01 01 01 06-91 321 11111111111 111 11111

CITICORP MORTGAGE/1000032037-020 REAL ESTATE
(01) XPN J 06-90 141000 1000 141000 07-91 CURRENT   00 00 00 07-91 11111111

PUBLIC RECORD INFORMATION
(00) BUT Courtand for Recordings:
(01) XPN CHAPTER 13 BANKRUPTCY FILED; DISMISSED 04-18-96; DN: 0000000, CO: F000000, CN: US BKPT CT TN JACKSON)

-------- END DEROGATORY ITEMS --------

Continued on page Two

Source: CreditReport.com

What Am I Looking for?

When you receive a copy of your credit report, you also receive instructions for interpreting the information on the report. Since each agency uses different information, pay close attention to special abbreviations and codes.

There are certain things you should look for in your credit file no matter which CRA provides the report. Always check for:

- **The name and address of the CRA that provided the report.** This is important because "TB3s" are huge; sometimes different addresses are used for certain departments. Start a phone/address log. You may need to contact more than one department of the bureau to settle a dispute. Having the proper address will ensure that the information gets into the right hands in a timely manner.

- **Your name, address, date of birth, and social security number.** If you have a common name (e.g. Tom Jones, Bob Smith or Sam Brown) or common address (e.g. Main Street, Martin Luther King Boulevard, or Breezy Lane), you could also have a common, but costly, mistake on your credit file — someone else's information.

- **The quantity and type of credit inquiries on your file.** There are industry standard credit inquiries. For example:

  ❖ A credit grantor you currently do business with reviews your file for a credit increase offer.

  ❖ Several inquiries may be logged by companies which you have *not* requested credit from, or in states other than yours. Be alert! Someone may be trying to get credit in your name.

- **Be aware of duplication accounts.** If you know that you closed an account, or paid it in full, there is no reason this account should appear active or open, while another says "Closed By Consumer." This should send up a RED FLAG to you because it sends one to a credit grantor reviewing your file. It could look as if you have too much credit, and hinder your chances of receiving a much deserved credit approval or increase.

- **Inaccurate account "opened" and "closed" dates** are a big problem and work against you so don't delay; if you see a date that you know is wrong, take action. CHALLENGE IT! If you opened your credit card account in 1995, but the report reflects that it was opened in 1997, this is not only inaccurate but also potentially damaging to your rating.

Now What?

So, you now have a copy of all three of your credit reports (or a "Three-in-One" report) and reviewed each one carefully. Now what? What do you do if the information is not correct? What are your rights? How do you get your questions answered?

Dispute Inaccurate Information with the CRA.

If you tell a CRA that your file contains inaccurate information, the CRA must investigate the items (usually within 30 days) by presenting to its information source all relevant evidence you submit, unless your dispute is frivolous.

The source must review your evidence and report its findings to the CRA. The source also must advise national CRAs, to which it has provided the data, of any error.

The CRA must give you a written report of the investigation and a new copy of your credit report if the investigation results in any change.

If the CRA firm's investigation does not resolve the dispute, you may add a brief statement to your file. The CRA must normally include a summary of your statement in future reports. If an item is deleted, or a dispute statement is filed, you may ask that anyone who has recently received your report be notified of the change. Source: FairCreditReportingAct.com

Seeing your credit report for the first time can be a shocker. Now that you know what you can do if the information is inaccurate, or not yours, understand this:

> *"A poor credit history that is accurate cannot be changed. There is nothing that you (or anyone else) can do to require a credit bureau to remove accurate information from your credit report until the reporting period has expired."[†]*

Although, the Fair Credit Reporting Act requires deletion of a negative entry that is inaccurate or unverifiable, total credit "clean-up" is a major misconception. So don't be fooled or tempted by companies with such claims.

For a full review of your rights as a credit consumer under the Fair Credit Reporting Act, visit www.faircreditreportingact.com or contact the Federal Trade Commission in writing or by phone:

Consumer Response Center — FCRA
Washington, DC 20580
(202) 326-3761

[†] Fair Credit Reporting Act

Ten Tips for Improving Your Credit

1. **Contact your credit card companies.** Make them aware of what's going on. If you inform them of your financial situation, it may help you in the long-term.

2. **Document EVERYTHING!** Try to do everything in writing. As it is said, "No paper? No proof."

3. **Trim the fat from your credit card.** Reduce your monthly expenses by canceling unnecessary services, protections, and offers.

4. **Request an interest rate reduction.** Or transfer your balance to a lower interest rate card. Contact your credit card company and request that they lower the interest you currently pay, or find a credit card company with a rate lower than your current credit card, and then switch.

5. **Don't try to get more credit.** Pay off what you have first, and commit to paying cash for all other purchases.

6. **Create a budget and stick to it.** The best rule to live by when creating a budget is to make it realistic.

7. **Systematically eliminate your credit cards.** Start by paying off the cards with the highest interest, not the highest balance.

8. **Check your credit report.** Request a copy of your report every six to eight months.

9. **Stop the credit madness.** Put an end to the flood of credit card offers. Call (888) 567-8688 to get your name removed from credit card company mailing lists.

10. **Be persistent and consistent** —
    Perseverance and hard work are the keys to
    regaining a creditworthy status.

The reality is, there are no quick fixes and no
magic wands to fix your credit. It will take time and
hard work. You might need to be uncomfortable now
to be creditworthy in the future.

Help, I'm In Too Deep!

If you are in the unfortunate state of feeling as if
you are drowning in debt and the suggestions offered
in the previous section seem like they aren't heavy-
duty enough for your circumstances, here's a bit of
information that might prove useful:

Collection Agencies — If your account has been
taken over by a collection agency, you will be
responsible to work with the new company contact to
settle your account.

There are laws that can protect you from being
harrassed, according to the Fair Credit Reporting Act
(FCRA) and the Fair Debt Collection Practices Act
(FDCPA).

According to the FDCPA here are some collection
agencies do's and don't's:

- A representative from the collection agency may
  contact you in person, by mail, phone, fax, or
  telegram.

- If you have an attorney (and have notified the
  collector of this fact), the collector must contact
  the attorney, rather than you personally.

- Collection agencies may *not* contact you before
  8:00 A.M. or after 9:00 P.M.

- Collection agencies may *not* contact you at unreasonable places, such as hospitals or rehabilitation facilities unless they have your prior consent.

- Collection agencies may *not* contact you at work if it is against your employer's rules for you to be contacted at work, or if you have told them that your employer does not approve of such contact.

- Within five days after you are first contacted, the debt collector must send you a written notice of the debt owed; how much, to whom, and what action you should take if you feel there has been an error.

- Collection agences are *not* to misrepresent themselves as agents of the government, attorneys, or as employees of the credit bureau. They also cannot use false personal or company names.

- Collection agencies are *not* allowed to make false statements. They cannot threaten jail time, nor state or imply that a crime has been committed. They also cannot threaten to garnish or withhold your wages.

- Collection agencies may *not* contact other people about you, except to find out where you live or work. They cannot reveal the nature of the call nor the amount of debt you owe.

- Collection agencies may *not* verbally abuse you, threaten you, or use profanity.

Although these laws have been written to protect you, they only work when you exercise your rights. If you feel your rights have been violated by a collection agency or its representative, it is in your best interest to report such wrong doings. Do not make the mistake of fighting with them or ignoring attempts to reach you. Such non-response could lead to a law suit against you.

To report such viloations, contact your Attorney General's office or the Federal Trade Commission. Put the request in writing and send a copy to the Federal Trade Commission as well as the creditor who hired the agency in question.

There are several ways to reach the Federal Trade Commissions Response Center:

- **Phone**: (877) 382-4357 (toll-free)

- **Regular Mail**: Federal Trade Commission
  CRC-240
  600 Pennsylvania Avenue NW
  Washington, DC 20580

- **Electronically**: You may fill out a complaint form at: www.ftc.gov/ftc/complaint.htm

If you feel you need help in contacting your creditors and negotiating lower monthly payments, contact a non-profit agency that specializes in helping debt-laden individuals.

One word of caution — NO ONE WILL CARE ABOUT YOUR FINANCIAL SITUATION LIKE YOU. Take the time to research companies that offer such services.

- Call the Better Business Bureau, for starters. There are several other watch-dog groups.

- Check their customer satisfaction rating.

- Ask the company for letters of reference and even permission to speak to satisified customers. If they are not willing to provide such information, you might want to consider a different agency.

How to Interview a Debt Agency:

The Federal Trade Commison suggests asking the following questions when researching debt agencies:

1. What specific services are offered?

2. After helping with your immediate debt needs, will they assist in developing a long-term plan for financial freedom?

3. Is there a service fee (many non-profits charge a fee)? If so, how much and how often do you pay? (Get general terms of agreement.)

4. Will a written contract be necessary? How long will you be required to work with them?

5. How soon will they begin working with you? How soon will you see results?

6. Who regulates or supervises the agency?

7. What type of credentials are their counselors required to have?

8. How many counselors will you work with? Will you be assigned a specific counselor?

9. Will your information remain confidential?

10. How are debt repayment amounts determined?

11. How does the repayment process work? Will you receive confirmation that your creditors have been paid as agreed?

12. Will status reports of your account be made available? If so, how often? Automatically, or upon request?

13. Can the agency get creditors to lower or eliminate interest rates and finance charges or waive late/over the limit fees?

14. What happens if you cannot maintain the agreed-upon plan?

15. Will any debts be excluded from the plan? If so, which ones and why? Is there a program the agency offers to help repay the excluded debts?

If working with an agency seems like an option you want to pursue, you can contact the National Foundation for Consumer Credit, which has a network of over 1,400 "Financial Care Centers" designed to help with debt management and repayment, bill payment, credit crisis resolution, counseling, and education. For more information, call (301) 589-5600, or visit www.nfcc.org for more information.

Understand that a debt consolidation company, counseling service, or debt repayment agency will not eliminate your previous credit history nor offer debt repayment loans. In fact, working with a third party to help with debt issues is likely to show up on your credit report and alert future creditors of your decision. This could influence a potential creditor's decision.

After several missteps, I chose to take on the challenge myself. It was very difficult, but, with so many negatives against me, and after realizing that few agencies had the power to do any more than I could do, I made the decision to do it myself.

I'll say it again, NO ONE WILL CARE ABOUT YOUR FINANCIAL SITUATION LIKE YOU.

— • ::⇥◆D◉◖◆⊱:: • —

6

HOW TO SURVIVE COLLEGE
ON A BUDGET

I will not try to convince you that creating and sticking to a budget is easy. It's simple, but not easy. It takes discipline. And who wants to be disciplined? I didn't, and neither do most people.

The word budget is one of the most dreaded. It's right up there with diet, root canal, and advanced calculus. A budget is not as bad as it seems, as with most things it's how we perceive it.

A funny thing happened when I realized that a budget is telling your money where to go, rather than wondering where it went. I was free from all the anguish I'd felt about having to live "on a leash." Moreover, truth be told, "You can't have the thrill without the bill." Eventually it'll catch up with you.

Now that it's been framed differently, allow me to paint a bigger picture. Unfortunately, no one has figured out how to run a college, company, or their personal life successfully without a well, thought-out plan. If you try, you might fool yourself into succeeding, but the house is betting against you, and the house always wins.

I've been where you are. I know how difficult it is: to be on your own, away from home, and introduced to a completely new freedom. The thought of putting restrictions on it just doesn't seem right. Freedom was the reason you went away to college in the first place. Right? True, but hear me on this. Credit cards can tempt you to live beyond your means. Think of the real freedom you'll

> *When you got to high school you thought, "Life begins in college." I'm here to tell you that you were only part right, "Life really begins after college!"*

have when you complete your education. In junior high you thought, "Life begins in high school." When you got to high school you thought, "Life begins in college." I'm here to tell you that you were only part right, "Life *really* begins after college!"

It does become tempting to try to live like your friends on campus, or like the ones back home that have not gone to college and have full time jobs. They will be getting things that you wish you had. However, try to keep it in perspective. The benefits of your education (the sacrifice) will pay off in just four short years. Your non-college friends may seem to have a lot now, but they won't have a college education.

Money does matter. If it didn't, you wouldn't be going to college. You've heard the statistics, read the reports that say, "Individuals with a college education make approximately 75% more in their lifetime than those with just a high school diploma do." Keep your eyes on the bigger prize. Life really begins after college; don't kill it before it starts. Here's how to keep it in check.

The Budgeting Process

Budgets are personal. We all have different expenses and needs. Just about any format will do, but, to create an effective budget, it's necessary to follow a few key steps.

1. **Put it on paper**. It's not good enough to have it in your head. List *all* of your regular expenses, from hair care to mobile phone bills, and everything in between.

   TIP: Don't create a miscellaneous column and put things like CDs and magazines in it. If you buy them on a regular basis, label them as "Entertainment."

2. Define your short-term goals. Do you want to party in South Beach for Spring Break? What about — get your car painted in the fall? Do you want to buy that special someone a great Christmas gift? Plan for it!

   TIP: You're in college; your main priority is school, but you can still have a little fun if you create a plan and stick to it.

3. Keep a mini version of your budget. Keep it in your wallet, purse, or wherever you'll see it. Review your goals each time you are considering making a non-budgeted purchase.

   TIP: "Out of sight, out of mind" should be your motto for your ex-boyfriend, not your budget. Reminding yourself that you're saving for Spring Break might be just the motivation you need not to overspend.

4. Track all spending. Getting to the checkout counter and finding out that you don't have any money isn't cool. Make sure you are aware of your cash standing at all times.

   TIP: Keep purchase receipts in the same section of your wallet as cash that way you'll have a running total of what you've spent and where. Also, check your bank balance regularly.

5. Avoid using the ATM. Don't use the ATM for more than the allowable number of "free transactions" per month.

   TIP: Always keep $20 to $50 in an easily accessible place and pull from your reserve before running to the ATM. Be sure to replace any borrowed money on your next visit.

6. Develop a radar for your money wasters (i.e. daily cups of coffee, cigarettes, eating out, snack/vending machines).

   TIP: If you're hitting the vending machine more than two times a week, you need to make a trip to the grocery store and get your snacks in bulk.

7. Cash is emotional, plastic is not. When deciding what purchases to put on your credit card, ask yourself, "Would I buy it if I had the cash?"

   TIP: When you use your card to purchase something new, the interest you accrue results in you paying three to five times more for the item than if you paid cash.

8. Commit to eliminating one money waster every semester.

   TIP: Late fees for video rentals, overdue library books, and parking tickets — all these add up. Get serious about keeping your money where it belongs, in your hands.

9. Save all of your change. Commit to putting all of your loose change in a jar. At the end of the semester, count the change. You'll be surprised how much you saved!

   TIP: Most banks or supermarkets have automatic change counters. When you figure out how much you have, put half toward your short-term goal and buy something that you know you've earned because of your new commitment to stick to a budget!

10. Allow room for treats, hobbies, and hanging out.

    TIP: If you're going to splurge, you might as well save. Visit www.coolsavings.com for discounts, deals, coupons, and freebies.

It's important to remain consistent and committed to the budget you've created. If you fail to restrain, modify, and deny yourself now, you will pay a dear price later. Remember, life really begins after college!

7

TEN WAYS TO MAKE MONEY IN COLLEGE: MONEYMAKING IDEAS TO GET PAID NOW

One of the most pressing issues on my mind (other than passing statistics class, figuring out what I was going to do for the weekend if I had to stay on campus, and what mystery meat was being served in the cafeteria) was how I could make some additional money in college.

Of course, there are the usual ways to make money, such as working at the mall, being a waiter, or even getting a job on campus. But, what are the alternatives? Entrepreneurship will be discussed in detail in chapter 16. Meanwhile, here are some great ways to make money in college.

What do you want more of other than money? While you could fill in the blank with all sorts of answers, I'd guess that time would be the one thing we can all agree on. Everyone is looking for someone to help do the things they hate to do, or have little time to do. Why not get paid for it?

Term Papers to Go: Remember that typing class you took in high school? If you were one of the few who "kept your eyes on your copy," you can now make money from those who didn't. Offer a service typing and delivering papers to your fellow students.

Of course, you need to determine what kind of value to put on such a service. Do you charge per word or a flat fee per paper? Would you offer research assistance as a service? How much would you charge for editing and proofreading? Make up some flyers, post them online and around campus and watch the business roll in. Be careful not to over commit yourself. Remember, you still have to type your own.

Streaming Lectures: Have you ever overslept and missed an important lecture, or tried to take notes during class but just couldn't keep up? If it hasn't happened to you, believe me, it has happened to your classmates. Leverage technology and make money at the same time. Record the lecture and offer to sell the copies, or allow students to download it from a password-protected Web site for a fee. This is no substitute for being in class, but it can really be a great service and revenue stream if you're in a jam.

(*Be sure to get prior approval from your professor, and college/university before capitalizing on this idea.*)

Handy Man Special: Get paid for what you love to do. Most of us grew up with computers, video games, and everything electronic. However, very few of us know what to do when they malfunction. If you are one of the unique individuals with the natural ability to fix things, or the ability to apply what you've read in the instructions manual, you can make money. Let people know that you can install, update, reassemble, and fix their radios, hairdryers, PDAs and PCs, and you'll be in high demand. Heck, you could become a millionaire by just programming the clocks on people's VCRs! (You can start with mine.)

The Human Browser: Information on the Internet is abundant. The key is finding what you need, when you need it, and in a timely fashion. We've all been there, looking for just the right word, statistic, or fact. Then, thirty minutes later, we're still trying to wade through the pile of "possible matches." You probably have a standard favorite search engine, but sometimes you need specialty tools. Develop a newsletter that offers tips, techniques and the URLs that people need to get the job done in a flash.

Go And Get It: If you attend college in a location where the Chinese restaurant doesn't deliver to the dorms after 10 P.M. (or not at all), you could make money and lots of it! Most of us have faced the dilemma of wanting Chinese food "after hours," forgetting to return the video and not feeling like leaving the house, or needing a bottle of Pepto-Bismol with no hope in sight.

If you have a car, or even a bike, you can have a business as a "gofer." It sounds silly, but you could be laughing all the way to the bank. Here's how: create a list of all the popular stores and restaurants in the area, develop a pick-up and delivery schedule, and determine your prices. Post the information and a contact number, and, when someone needs Chinese food at 11PM (you can also charge an "after hours fee") or a gallon of milk and cereal, you can come to the rescue.

Grooming Services 'R Us: Can you braid, cut, weave, perm, color, or style hair? Can you file, paint, or airbrush nails? Can you sew, knit, or make clothes?

All of these things are potential moneymakers on a college campus full of students that want to look good away from home. What's your unique talent? Would others benefit from it? Showcase your talents, let a few students try it out, and build a client base from there. The best advertising is word of mouth, so always give your best effort and they'll keep coming back.

Co-Ed Clean Up: I wonder how many of my friends and fellow students ever made it through college with their rooms and apartments such a mess. Most people aren't really slobs; they just choose to use their time on other things rather than cleaning.

If you have the ability to keep a neat room, own a mop, duster, and a broom or vacuum, why not get paid for cleaning? Offer your services to clean, make the bed, and disinfect the refrigerator of your fellow students. There's money to be made in a pile of dirty dishes!

Determine what your services will include (i.e. if you offer to wash clothes be very specific about that you'll wash-no undergarments) and how much you'll charge for each service. Offer free estimates and throw-in a complementary service (i.e. ironing or folding washed clothes). You'll be paid, and the campus will be a cleaner and better smelling place to live!

Pay per Use: Have you ever needed a book, but only for a few hours? What about a laptop for a day? Or, maybe, you needed a beeper or cell phone for a weekend? If you have ever been faced with the dilemma of needing something that you don't have or can't get, you know how frustrating it can be.

What if you turned that frustration into a business? There are many ways to capitalize on the concept of "Rent for a Day," or "Use For An Hour." Determine what people want and need, and then become the go-to guy or girl for their needs.

Of course, you'll have to develop guidelines for use i.e.: what condition the item must be in when returned, cost per hour (i.e. bulk rate discounts and late fees), and policies and procedures (hold their student ID card in exchange for use of your item), but the fun part will be connecting people with what they need.

Dialing for Dollars‡: Phoning home is one of the most important and expensive things you'll do while in college. In fact, according to Student Monitor Report, in a typical month college students make nearly 15 long distance calls. Keeping in touch with friends and family, and connecting with new acquaintances, is very important. Sure, e-mail is nice, but sometimes just hearing the other person's voice is just what the doctor ordered.

Reaching out and touching someone isn't always cheap. However, there are some great affiliate and referral marketing opportunities available. They allow you to help friends and family stay connected for a reasonable rate while you make money.

P2P Marketing: You're already endorsing Nike®, telling all your friends about the hot new PlayStation® game, or begging anyone who'll listen to try McDonald's® new milk shake, and don't forget about the message you posted praising the new Dell® notebook computer you recently purchased, so why not get paid to do it? Have you ever been told, "You should work for them," because you talk about a particular company's product or service so often?

Why not follow that advice, in a manner of speaking? Companies are always looking for non-traditional ways to boost sales and gain new consumers. You can help. To find out more about P2P marketing, log on to your favorite company's Web site and look around for information. If you don't find anything, gain a little inspiration from Luke McCabe and Chris Barrett — two college students who are paying for their education by promoting companies' products. For more info, go to www.chrisandluke.com.

---

‡ Source: www.cdcresources.com

Cash In On the Web: The Internet has exploded since I was in college, never before has there been such a powerful and inexpensive way to market yourself, a product, or just your ideas.

To establish your online presence, you need two things.

1. You need a domain name. Choose something that will be easy to remember and relate to what you're offering.

2. You need a host for the domain name. This will ensure that you can share your Web site with the world. For a low cost, all-inclusive package, visit: www.noexcusesdomains.com for details.

Launch your moneymaking idea on the web today!§

— • ::⇌◆ɔ○Є◆⇌:: • —

---

§ Ideas in this section are merely suggestions and are not intended to be used if they are in any way a violation to university policies or illegal in your state. Author assumes no responsibility for the outcome of the use of ideas contained herein.

Section B

CRACK 'DA CODE ON
LOVE

If you think understanding money matters seems difficult, try figuring out love!

I am including a section about love in a book primarily about money and careers because, unbelievably, love plays a big part in how much money you make and keep, where you work and how you live.

College is an awesome experience. For many who venture off to college, it's the first time to make your own decisions, to test your street smarts, and to define the world on your own terms. It is, truly, the best of times, and it is the worst of times.

Being in love in college adds a completely new dimension to the college experience. Often, our emotions cloud our judgment. We buy into the belief that, if someone loves us, they will prove it by spending money on us.

I spent a lot of time and money in college trying to use money (actually, credit cards — that you now know aren't the same as money) to prove my love for others and myself. The result: I was frustrated and broke, and I didn't marry any of the men I spent lots of money on!

Love is confusing enough without the complications of money. Don't assume that money will buy love or that it is a measure of someone's love for you. Read on, to crack 'da code on love.

8

LOVE GAMES YOU SHOULD NEVER PLAY

One of the best things about college for me was making new friends. People from different backgrounds and states fascinated me. I was impressed with the older students and intrigued by my classmates. The vast array of ethnically diverse people was amazing. It was a playground — a rainbow of colors and smells and people!

The fascination quickly turned to puzzlement, as I tried to figure out how to get to know these people, especially the boys.

Now, although I am a woman, I want to address both sexes in this section of the book. I've gained insight from both perspectives, and I think you'll find there's value in what I have to say.

Stick with me on this one, as I use popular songs to make my point. You just might learn a thing or two about playing games and being played. At the very least, you'll be entertained.

There's a song that says, "People make the world go 'round." It's true. They do. Unfortunately, most of the time, they go around confused about the people who are making it go around!

What's Love Got to Do with It?

In 1989, Tina Turner, the sultry singer with the sexy legs, sang a song that set the airwaves on fire. Soon after its release, everyone was asking the question posed in the song, "What's love got to do with it?"

While Tina sings of the conflicting emotions of being *in love* verses *in lust,* the question begs to be asked, as it relates to this section of the book; What does love have to do with money and the dream job?

Actually quite a bit. The beginning stages of love are full of butterflies, long talks, and romantic dinners, but somewhere along the way money comes into play.

Usually, money's entrance is casual and innocent. It shows up in the awkwardness of deciding if you'll split the bill. However, fast-forward in time when the first date jitters are long gone. You could quickly experience the frustration of being with someone who has no regard for money and whose priorities seem to be out of line with the reality of your finances.

Lesson: Ask the tough money questions early, and know what you're getting into. Even if you don't consider the person you are dating "marriage material," it is very important to know their money type. Are you a "saver" dating a "spender?" Or, are both of you "spenders?"

Love has a lot to do with it because you marry your spouse's debt, and according to The Divorce Statistic Collection survey, you are 25% less likely to get married and 60% more likely to get divorced due to bad debt.

Oops, I Did It Again

It was an unusually warm spring day and I was walking across campus to the only building that seemed to have kicked into summer AC mode. I hurried along, quickly thinking about the cool breeze and little else, when I heard a "psst" sound.

Being that it was Virginia in the spring, it could have been a bug, so I kept walking.

Again, I heard it, this time in triplicate "psst," "psst," "psst." It could have been a bug, but it turned out to be a pest (of the male species).

Now listen, guys, trying to get a girls attention with, "psst," "shorty," "yo," "hey," "you girl," "boo," "hottie," "cutie," or with the one-finger "come hither" move, or any other smooth move is tacky. If you happen to get their attention (or even their number), you might want to think twice.

After talking with — shall we call him James? I was as annoyed as I was intrigued by his take on the college experience. Against my better judgment, I agreed to meet him after class for pizza.

The entire time we were eating, I was thinking about how completely corny he was; how he wasn't my "type" (as if I'd figured out my type). But he had one thing going for him — he had cash, or at least enough to buy the pizza and offer to take me to the movies later. I figured it would be harmless to go out with him a few times. Why not?

We hung out for the next few weeks, going to the movies, the game room, and even "the sweat box" — our gym turned into an on-campus club on Friday nights with far too little air circulation (so much so, that after one song everyone is covered in sweat). For me, hanging with him was a distraction; something to do.

However, I couldn't say the same applied for him. I knew that he liked me as more than a friend, but I played dumb every time the subject came up. I admit that I was sending mixed signals. For the record I'm not proud of this, but I want to tell you, so you won't play this game or get played.

After about two months of this cat and mouse game, I was caught and it wasn't pretty! I fought back tears as James called me exactly what I was — "A tease" (and some other colorful language, as I'm sure you can imagine) and threw me out of his car in front of my dorm (I deserved worse).

I hurt a really nice guy. I used him. I did not intend to be anything more than friends . . . and who needs a friend like that. I played dumb when I knew he liked me.

Worst of all, at that moment, I had no remorse. I never gave a second thought to how I would feel if the tables were turned, or how I would get myself out of the tangled web I had spun.

Lesson: College is a time of testing the waters, trying things, and exploring new options, but it is also a time to mature and grow. Don't play games with peoples' emotions.

If you have no interest in the other person, be straight with them. It might seem innocent to "play with your heart, get lost in the game," as Britney Spears sings it in "Oops! . . . I Did It Again," but you are dealing with a real person and it is not a game!

Admitting you were wrong is very difficult. Saying you're sorry is even harder. But, remember that what goes around truly comes back around. Innocent or not, it won't feel like an "Oops!" when it's happening to you.

Who's Zoomin' Who?

In 1985, Aretha Franklin, the Queen of Soul, sang a song about the games we play when we're playing with the opposite sex.

Holding on to one person while you're waiting for someone better to come around is not only stupid, it's wrong. The chances of your deception being discovered are big.

Leaving high school sweethearts behind is one of the most difficult parts of adjusting to college life. Saying goodbye to your friends, but especially your boy or girlfriend, can be hard to do. Most of the time we are convinced that we can continue to remain the same person we were and still have the same relationship that we had in school. Very rarely is that the case, even with the best intentions.

I learned this lesson the painful way when I found out that the guy I was seeing had a girl he'd been friends with at home. But he said he "really liked me, too." I couldn't be too angry because even though we were "seeing" each other, I still maintained a very close connection with my old boyfriend.

I liked the newness of Zion but longed for the uncomplicated and comfortable relationship I had with Paul. We were playing each other and trying not to get caught. However, the heart rarely does what the mind tells it to; we found ourselves liking each other in the present, while trying to stay connected with the past.

It was difficult to sort out all of the emotions because, while we both understood what was going on, it made it no less complicated or painful to realize that our hearts were not truly free.

Lesson: The lyrics "It's So Hard to Say Goodbye to Yesterday" of the Boys II Men song are true. But it is necessary to do so. The scary and exciting thing about change is that it requires things to, well, change! We tend to want to hold on to the familiar while our human nature longs to gravitate to what's new and different.

Branch out: spread your wings and allow your friends back home to do the same. Give them (and yourself) the space and permission to move on. It will seem difficult and awkward for a while, but the transition will be so much smoother at the beginning than explaining to your boy or girlfriend that you "want to see other people" in the end.

The Boy (Or Girl) Is Mine

I love how life can be so neatly put into song, but how very different it can seem and feel when we're living the experience that's being strung over a cool beat.

Monica and Brandy, arguably the new divas of R&B, hit the airwaves the summer of 1998 with the coolest catfight of the century. "The Boy Is Mine" pitted Brandy against Monica as they defended their positions for loving the same man. Brandy called Monica "insane" as Monica called Brandy "blind," and all the while, both were obviously being played.

Lesson: He's not worth fighting over, and neither is she! You deserve to be with someone who wants to be with you and who will be honest with you. There is nothing romantic about being caught in an emotional tug of war between someone who isn't mature enough to make up his or her mind. Confronting the person who is playing games with your heart (and not the person you're accusing them of cheating on you with) will be painful, but necessary. You will feel exhilarated and dignified as you let them know that you are aware of the games they've been playing, and remove yourself gracefully from the equation.

Believe me: your self-respect and self worth are priceless. The way that you represent yourself is key to building your character and others' perception of you. My grandmother and a popular country song from the '90s said it best: "If you stand for nothing, you'll fall for anything."

Down for Whatever

Hormones raging, music blasting, the moon beaming . . . that was the atmosphere one cool night in September. The semester had just started and everyone was out in the parking lot having a good time.

I had my eye on a very cute boy, and he was matching my stare. I walked over and introduced myself. We exchanged niceties and numbers. One of us promised to call the other and I drifted back to be with my girls.

I called him later that night. We talked (actually he talked — saying all the "right things") and agreed to hook-up later in the week.

Over the four days between our initial meeting and seeing each other again, we spoke everyday and the conversations lasted longer and longer each time. By the time we connected in person, I told him that I felt like I knew him and he told me he loved me! (How that's possible when we'd known each other for only a week, escapes me.)

I was on Cloud Nine, and stayed there, until I found out that the love was conditional. When he learned that I wasn't "down for whatever" the "love" quickly changed to something a lot less beautiful.

When I asked him, why he said that he loved me, he answered,

"I did love you, when I said it."

Pleeeze . . .

Maybe he believed that or maybe he thought I was naïve. I guess both are true.

Lesson: Love is complicated and multi-layered. We have boiled it down to a feeling that comes and goes, as often as the sun rises and sets. Don't say you love someone if you don't. Don't confuse butterflies in your stomach, dizziness, and shortness of breath with love — it was probably a bad reaction to yesterday's lunch.

I don't mean to be flippant, but here's the real deal. Rarely can you make a strong statement such as "I love you" when you've only known someone for a few short weeks, let alone days. Infatuation is real, it's powerful, and so is physical attraction. It is not, however, love.

No More Drama

I've only scratched the surface on the love games that we play, but I hope I gave a vivid picture of the reality of the hurt that the games can produce.

Mary J. Blige sings of love and pain, sunshine and rain in the song "No More Drama." She sings about knowing yourself: about removing the negativity and stress. She sings of freedom from the drama that we allow (yes, we actually choose drama) to invade and often consume our lives.

College is a time for growth and self-actualization: a time to work on *you*. Do unto others, as you would have them do unto you. I know this seems old fashion, but you'd be surprised how much less drama you'll attract by living by this golden rule. Learn to spend time with, and get to know, yourself. Too many times I tried to get friends to fill the voids. Little did I realize, I had a lot of growing to do myself.

Lesson: You have more control than you realize. Examine your circumstances and truly ask yourself how much of the hurt, stress, and frustration you are experiencing is in your power to change. I bet that ridding your life of toxic friends, negative beliefs, bad choices, and drama can eliminate more than 90 percent of the pain.

— • ::═╬●ɔơɕ●╋═:: • —

Section C

CRACK 'DA CODE TO
THE DREAM JOB

Making it through college is no small feat. According to ACT, almost 26% of students who start college do not finish. You should be excited if your college experience is ending.

Unfortunately, just when you've started to figure it out, it's time to enter a new and uncertain phase of life.

There are so many options after college. Maybe you will have the opportunity to take some downtime and travel, or spend time volunteering. However, at some point, you will need to consider how you plan to apply your college degree.

This section of the book is full of tips, information, and advice to help you make sense of the world of work. Use it as a resource as your life begins after college.

9

LANDING A HOT INTERNSHIP: THE TEST DRIVE

I majored in Mass Communications in college. I went from wanting to be an anchor, to a radio personality, to a marketing executive, to a music mogul. Fortunately, I had some very perceptive people helping me to see that anything is possible, but not all possibilities were ideal.

The popular radio station where I went to college was located downtown just a short trip away from campus. More than anything, I wanted (or so I thought) to be heard by thousands of my fellow students announcing the top ten hits of the day, playing jokes on callers, and having fun on the airwaves. So, just before the spring semester of my sophomore year ended, I called the radio station and asked about their internship opportunities at the station. I was told that the deadline for internships had passed but that I could send my resume anyway.

I was discouraged, but I sent in my resume. About three weeks later, I got a call from the station saying that there was a morning drive, newsroom internship position available.

Now, news in the morning wasn't my idea of fun, but I really wanted to be on the radio, and I had received some wise advice from my advisor; "Get in the door, anyway you can."

I went on the interview and landed the internship! I'm not sure if I got it because no one else wanted it, or because no one else applied. I didn't care; I was ecstatic! I was going to be in radio. That was my entrance into internships and to the benefit of the "test drive."

The lessons I learned that semester were invaluable. The first thing I realized very quickly was why I got the internship. No one wanted to get up at 4:30 A.M., be to work by 5:00 A.M., and pull news off the wire for a 6:00 A.M. news program (which you got no credit for!). The adjustment period was difficult. What kept me there, more than pride (I'm not a quitter), were the off-air lessons.

Stan "The Man," "Chase-Commander 'N Chief of The Base," Cheryl and "Doc" were a few of the morning radio personalities that taught me the real lessons of radio. The most profound of which: you have to pay your dues.

Before interning at the radio station, I was convinced that I would be in radio. Everyone told me I had a great voice. My course load leaned toward radio, and I was on my way . . . or so I thought. Often we have unrealistic expectations and the best way to prevent those

A combination of things led me to realize that radio was not for me.
However, the experience was priceless.

expectations from leading us in the wrong direction is by "kicking the tires" and trying it out for ourselves.

A combination of things led me to realize that radio was not for me. However, the experience was priceless. Not only did it help me figure out what I didn't want to do, it also challenged me to look at other possibilities.

When considering which career you'd like to leave your mark on, it's ok to change your mind a few times. Many factors will help you decide if you're suited to be in the profession you're pursuing. However, don't let a personality conflict or a bad experience be your only deciding factor.

The best method I've found, after figuring out what classes are required to get the degree, is the "test drive," also known as an internship. Most companies have active programs that hire and invest in internship candidates; it's a win-win situation. You get a feel for the industry, and what it's like to do the job, and the company gets low cost labor and a possible future employee.

10

HOW TO APPLY FOR AN INTERNSHIP

An internship can be viewed as a beginning step to a career, rather than just another job. I say this to stress the difference in applying for an internship verses a job. There are several things to consider and be prepared for.

In most cases, your internship experience will be an opportunity to show potential employers that you have had real world experience and have given forethought to your future.

I cannot stress enough that timing is key. The internship process could take as little as three weeks, or more typically six to eight weeks, from the receipt of your resume and application to being placed with a company.

Step 1: Research

There are several resources available to research internships. Consider using your favorite Internet search engine to identify companies in your industry of study. Also, consider purchasing a resource guide from Kaplan or Peterson's. I prefer this source because the information provided in resource guides tends to be better focused and easy to use.

The goal of your research should be to:

- Identify companies of interest.

- Learn candidate selection criteria.

- Determine application process timeline.

Step 2: Resume & Application

Your resume introduces you to potential employers, but realize the introduction will be brief — very brief. Your resume will be scanned at best. It's important that it be well organized, easy to read and follow, no more than one page, and accurate (avoid the temptation to embellish).

You can take advantage of several resources when preparing your resume. Again, the Internet is an awesome source of information. Type "resume" in your favorite browser and you'll get a host of options. There are several resume styles. However, remember that you'll only have one chance to make a good impression, so know your audience. Attempting to impress a conservative company representative with an "over-the-top" resume might not be the best option.

In addition, many companies will receive your resume on-line. If you choose this option, be sure to convert the file to PDF or "text only" file to avoid text-formatting distortion when the receiver opens the file.

At minimum, include standard information, such as:

- **Identification** — Name, current address (both school and permanent), phone number, and e-mail. Be sure that you choose a professional e-mail name. Pookiebear@crazyhorse.com is not an appropriate e-mail address for a resume.

- **Education** — Name of high school and college or university, degrees earned, graduation date, and major/minor areas of study.

- **Experience** — Try to make this relevant experience. If you work at a convenience store, for instance, how can you relate the experience to your targeted career?

- **Activities** — Only include if your activities are relevant to the job you are seeking. List the most relevant first.

- **Honors** — This gives you an opportunity to highlight your accomplishments and achievements.

- **References** —According to professional resume writers, it is not even necessary to include "Available upon request." But be aware that they will be requested if you are considered for employment. Be sure to make copies of recommendation letters for future use.

Many companies require you to submit an application in addition to a resume. Your research of the company will determine if that is necessary. Most applications are available on the company's Web site and are easy to download.

Step 3: Your Cover Letter

In most cases, the representative from the company you are applying to will see your resume before meeting you. A cover letter can be the virtual handshake or icebreaker. Allow your unique personality to shine through in the cover letter. Use it as an opportunity to highlight specific information in your resume and draw attention to experiences that will make you a suitable candidate.

When constructing your cover letter, be sure to address the letter in the correct formal manner and include:

- Your address.

- Representative information (name, title, address).

- Date.

- A "purpose paragraph" expressing your purpose for writing and your interest in the position offered. (Be sure to match each letter to a specific position if possible.)

- A paragraph highlighting your relevant past experiences, accomplishments, and achievements.

- A conclusion paragraph detailing how and when you can be contacted, your follow-up plan.

- Finally, thank the representative for their time and consideration.

Proofread your resume and cover letter several times. Ask a professor, career counselor, and friend to review it as well. You cannot afford to send an ill-prepared resume to speak on your behalf!

Step 4: The Interview

Preliminary Phone Interview:

Prepare for the interview by making an appointment with the campus career counselor and conducting a mock interview. Be sure to have your resume to get valuable feedback. Your research will let you know if an in-person interview is required. Most companies will opt to conduct a preliminary phone interview before scheduling an in-person interview.

If you are scheduled for a phone interview, be sure to choose a quiet location, disable call waiting, and speak directly into the phone. It is easy to get the wrong impression of someone over the phone since you only have your hearing to rely on.

When being interviewed over the phone, be sure to speak clearly and slowly. Put a smile in your voice and on your face. (Sometimes looking at yourself in a mirror is helpful so you can see yourself in conversation.) Stand-up during the phone interview, standing will ensure that your voice is projected because you can breathe better.

Be prepared to speak about your abilities, long-term career goals, and potential contributions to their company. Think about the questions that they may ask you. For example, what are your strengths/weaknesses? What do you expect to gain and learn from your internship? Why should they choose you over the other applicants? Be sincere and be honest. Do your homework and don't underestimate the competition.

You should view the interview as a two-way communication process. Ask questions that will give you a better understanding of the corporate culture, as well as the experience overall. Prepare questions in advance and be sure they are well thought out.

In-person Interview — Attire and Appearance

While it is illegal to discriminate on the bases of race, gender, religion, and sexual orientation, companies have the right to be discriminating when it comes to what they deem "appropriate appearance/attire." There is no denying that people make judgment calls based on appearance whether appropriate or not.

College is a time of personal expression; many students get their first piercing done, or venture into getting tattoos during the college experience. Regardless of the image you choose to adopt for your personal life, realize that even in the 21st century, it is usually not appropriate to venture too far from traditional, borderline-conservative attire for an interview.

Unless you have first hand knowledge of a more lax dress code, then opt for a traditional suit for men and a pant or skirt suit for women — better safe, than sorry. You will never hear that you weren't called back for a second interview because you were dressed inappropriately. Unfortunately, it happens more than companies are willing to admit.

Remove any visible piercing and attempt to cover tattoos by wearing long sleeve shirts, slacks, and dark stockings or pantyhose. Skirts should be no more than an inch above the knee when seated (You'll feel and look awkward if you find it necessary to continue adjusting your skirt during the interview.).

In-person Interview — Etiquette

When you meet the company representative in person for the first time, be sure to:

- Offer a solid handshake (limp handshakes denote weakness).

- Make eye contact during the handshake and the interview.

- Be an attentive listener (focus on the person asking the question, not the question being asked).

- Answer questions concisely and directly.

- Don't be afraid to ask for clarification of a question when necessary (You'll look more intelligent if you ask before answering a question that you don't understand.)

- When appropriate, reinforce your specific qualifications.

- Get a clear understanding of the position (will college credit be given, how many hours are required).

- Discuss follow-up procedures and next steps (Should you contact them, or wait to be contacted?)

- Thank the interviewer and be sure to leave any necessary paperwork for further review.

Within a week of the interview, send a thank-you note via snail mail — it's more personal than e-mail (be sure to reference the date of the interview and position you interviewed for).

Step 5: Written Expectations

Most companies have a formal internship program with an outline of goals and responsibilities, however to ensure that you get the most from your experience it might be helpful to create your own outline. Consider the following:

- How many hours per day will you work per day and week?

- If college credit is not given, attempt to arrange an alternate.

- What specifically do you want to learn (list at least three targeted things)?

- What will your performance evaluation be based on?

- Determine boundaries: are you able to volunteer to help in other departments; work over-time hours?

By clearly defining your goals in the beginning, you have a better chance of a well-rounded and productive learning experience.

———— ►·ᴴ═◄♦)⊙(♦⁝═ᴴ·◄ ————

11

FIVE WAYS TO LAND
A HOT INTERNSHIP

1: Be Prepared

Most companies have Web sites with a section dedicated to human resources and employment opportunities. Research the internship requirements and be mindful of the deadlines and rules.

NOTE: Ask professors and advisors for letters of recommendation, and get copies of transcripts in advance. Give yourself at least three weeks to gather all necessary documents before they're due. In addition, due to time constraints, have a letter (or at least a template) written that can be reviewed, edited, and signed by the professor.

TIP: When you ask for a letter of recommendation, be sure you've established a rapport with the professor *before* you ask. Be prepared to give all the pertinent information necessary to process the request. Include:

- The person/company to be addressed
- Your accomplishments and activities
- Your major, graduation year and GPA

2: Be Open to the Possibilities

Someone once said, "The best gifts come in dull packages." If you don't get one of the coveted internships in the department you want, look for other alternatives to learn and grow.

NOTE: Apply to at least five internship programs, more if possible. It's better to have too many options than not enough.

TIP: I learned more about how a radio station runs from my mentor in the newsroom than all of the interns combined. Why? Because I was willing to do a job that few wanted. As a result, I gained the attention of the person in charge. A high profile internship doesn't always mean: great learning experience.

3: Network

Join the student chapter of key professional organizations in your field of interest.

NOTE: This is a great way to develop your social and business skills, and begin to build a database for the future. It also looks great on your resume.

TIP: Knowing individuals that are willing to "keep an eye out" for you can be priceless when seeking an internship or a job.

4: Be Pleasantly Persistent

There's a fine line between being a pest and being persistent. Respect the hiring manager's time and preferences (i.e. if a person prefers e-mail to phone calls, respect that). Create a follow-up plan at the time of interview and state your intentions to follow-up. Be thorough.

NOTE: Familiarize yourself with the person's assistant or coordinator. They can prove to be a valuable source of information and support.

TIP: Break through the clutter. When following up, send at least one correspondence via regular mail (i.e. a thank you note). It's more personal and will gain attention, especially if you choose a colored envelope.

5: Market Yourself

If you feel you are a good candidate for the position, let it show. Advertise and market your abilities and do so in a creative way. Marketers face the challenge of breaking through the clutter to get the decision maker's attention — your mission is the same.

NOTE: Sometimes people can suffer from technology overload. Too many e-mails, voice mails, and an endless barrage of electronic signals can make a person numb. Send thank you notes and follow-up correspondence via regular mail.

TIP: Go for the unconventional. When sending correspondence, use bright colored envelopes and address the package by hand.

12

WHAT TO DO ONCE YOU'RE IN

- Commit to being professional, no matter how relaxed the environment might seem. Being professional is more a state of mind then a matter of dress. Watch your language, your tone, and your mannerisms. Believe it or not, people are watching you.

- Recognize and realize that you'll have to prove yourself worthy of people's time and attention. You'll probably be sitting in a cubicle rather than a corner office — all eyes will be on you. Don't allow downtime to make you seem lazy and uninvolved. Volunteer to help in all areas of the department. There are dues to be paid and you never know who'll remember your willingness to step up to the plate.

- Make a point to talk to as many people as possible. I can't stress enough that you never know who is watching. Be polite, responsive, and courteous to everyone (especially those you might be tempted to disregard).

- Stand out — be noticed. There's a fine line between being an over zealous neophyte and someone who's eager and willing to learn. Be available and responsible and people will notice you.

- Be sure to complete the small tasks before expecting to be assigned the big ones.

- Sometimes working without pay is worth more than being paid, especially if the tradeoff is knowledge. If there's an opportunity to help on a project after hours or on the weekend, take it. It could be the catalyst you need to acquire paid employment in the future.

- Identify a mentor. A mentor is someone whose work and style you admire. A mentor is not always the most seemingly high profile person. A mentor could be someone who can help explain to you the unspoken rules of the company, or someone with years of experience in the industry that can offer a history of where it's been and a synopsis of where it's going.

- Beware of the company you keep. Avoid office gossip, no matter how "juicy" or appropriate it might seem. Gossips are never regarded highly.

So, you've tested the waters and found what you want to do with the rest of your life. The journey is just beginning. Here are a few things I learned about the illusive "dream job."

———— ▸◂═━◂◆◐◖◗◆▸═━◂ ◂ ————

13

YOUR INCOME
VS.
YOUR SALARY

Boy, was I in for a rude awakening when I left college. All my life my parents told me that if I were college educated, I would have access to the best jobs and that those jobs would equal lots of money. While this is true, I was never taught a time frame in which to expect to get paid "lots of money." Therefore, I naturally assumed this would happen immediately.

We live in a world of contradictions. On television, we see the good life, we see well-dressed people going to exciting and fulfilling jobs that they love while driving expensive cars and smiling. We see ultra rich celebrities throwing lavish parties and drinking $250 bottles of champagne.

Rarely do we see life, as we know it. Hard working people concerned about which bills to pay and questioning whether they will be able to go on vacation. We pursue education for a better life, and rightfully so — however, the picture that is portrayed on TV is far from the true income reality. According to the 2000 Census, the average American family had a median income of $35,691 and the median income of a non-family was $21,861.

I stress income vs. salary because few people really grasp the difference until they are challenged to live on the income and not the salary. My first job in New York City paid a salary of $27,000. I was a bit disappointed when I heard the number. I assumed that as a college grad I would be making at least $50,000, but I figured I could make it work, at least until my first raise or promotion; another rude

> *Few people really grasp the difference until they are challenged to live on the income and not the salary.*

awakening. I started doing the math oblivious to the bite taxes would take out of me.

A $27,000 salary in New York equaled a $19,000 income — OUCH! That really hurt. Plus, I was $15,000 in debt. In a perfect world, I could have paid off all of my debt and lived off $4,000 for the year. However, I had all of these other pesky little expenses like a rent of $12,000/year ($1,000 per month to live in an apartment the size of a jail cell — you've gotta love New York!). Food was necessary. Utilities were important. Professional clothes were a must. I probably spent $1,000 alone on panty hose! And for you guys, don't think you won't spend just as much on dry cleaning those shirts that Mom isn't around to iron. Then of course, there is the social life I wanted to have. Quite the dilemma on the income I made.

A salary is the dollar amount your employer agrees to pay you; an income is what Uncle Sam allows you to live on. Two very different things — don't get it twisted!

Why is your paycheck so small you might ask? Here's why.

You have before-tax salary commonly referred to as gross income; and after-tax income known as net income. Net income is what is left to live on, after the federal government takes its share from each employee. Deductions include Social Security tax, federal tax, state tax, and local income tax. Other deductions may appear on your pay stub depending on the state in which you live.

Deductions are taken based on the answers you provide when filling out your W-4 form. This form is required by all employers in order to track your wages and taxes owed. The purpose of this form is to determine the withholding allowances for which you are eligible. The more allowances you take, the less income will be withheld. Standard allowances cover martial status, parental status and home ownership.

Withholdings operate on a deduct-as-you-go system. As an employee, your employer is obligated to withhold taxes during your employment period.

A breakdown of the taxes you'll pay will help you understand where your money goes when you enter the work world.

Social Security and Medicare

Although tax laws change frequently, the following are the percentages of your wages that fund your retirement and keep the government in business.

- Social Security tax is the government managed retirement income fund for persons 65 and older, 6.2% of your income goes to Social Security.

- Medicare or government managed health care accounts for 1.45% of your income.

This equals a total contribution of 7.65% of your gross income. The good news is that your employer matches that percentage on your behalf to help fund your retirement.

Tax Bracket Withholdings

You might have heard the phrase "tax bracket" or "tax rate." This refers to the tax perimeters set by the federal government. A "graduated" or sliding scale system is used to calculate taxes. Each bracket contains an income range and also has an equivalent rate.

All of this can be quite confusing because there is also something called "the marginal tax rate," which is the rate that your "last dollar gets taxed." The marginal rate is the highest rate at which any of your money is taxed. In 2002, there were six tax brackets:

Tax Brackets—2002 Taxable Income[**]

Joint return	Single taxpayer	% Rate
$0–$12,000	$0–$6,000	10.0
$12,000–46,700	$6,000–27,950	15.0
$46,700–112,850	$27,950–67,700	27.0
$112,850–171,950	$67,700–141,250	30.0
$171,950–307,050	$141,250–307,050	35.0
$307,050 and up	$307,050 and up	38.6

Federal taxes take the largest chunk of your tax payment.

State and Local Withholdings

You'll also need to factor in approximately 5–7% of your gross income for state and local taxes. You can

[**] Source: Tax Foundation

see how my $27,000 salary quickly dwindled down to a net income of $19,000. The reality of taxes was almost more painful than being $15,000 in debt!

When you begin your career after college, it's a good idea to plan a meeting with your company's human resources contact. They can provide answers to questions relating to deductions, withholdings, and other income saving strategies such as 401k plans.

————— ►·⸬═⸫◆⊃◉€◆⸬═·⸬─◄ —————

14

STARTING SALARIES — WHAT COLLEGE STUDENTS REALLY GET PAID

I entered the world of work with a level of ignorance. I did not realize the starting salaries paid to college graduates. Had I known that my net income would equal the amount of my outstanding debt load, I'm sure I would have made different choices.

Unfortunately, in the 21st century race and gender still matter. As a nation, we have made great strides in pay equality regardless of the ethnicity of the employee. However, the gaps between men vs. women and white vs. black still exist.

According to a "Median Annual Earnings by Race and Sex" report published by The National Committee on Pay Equity, there are still disparities that need to be addressed.

2000 Median Annual Earnings by Race and Sex[tt]

Race/gender	Earnings	Wage ratio
White men	$38,869	100%
White women	$28,080	72%
Black men	$30,409	78%
Black women	$25,117	64%
Hispanic men	$24,638	63%
Hispanic women	$20,527	52%
All men	**$37,339**	
All women	**$27,355**	
Wage gap		**73%**

Another report published by the same group took the study further by showing the gains made in income and race over the past 30 years.

The Wage Gap, by Gender and Race[tt]

Year	White men	Black men	Hispanic men	White women	Black women	Hispanic women
1970	100%	69.0%	N/A	58.7%	48.2%	N/A
1975	100%	**74.3%**	72.1%	57.5%	55.4%	49.3%
1980	100%	70.7%	70.8%	58.9%	55.7%	50.5%
1985	100%	69.7%	68.0%	63.0%	57.1%	52.1%
1990	100%	73.1%	66.3%	69.4%	62.5%	54.3%
1992	100%	72.6%	63.3%	70.0%	64.0%	55.4%
1994	100%	75.1%	64.3%	71.6%	63.0%	55.6%
1995	100%	75.9%	63.3%	71.2%	64.2%	53.4%
1996	100%	80.0%	63.9%	73.3%	65.1%	56.6%
1997	100%	75.1%	61.4%	71.9%	62.6%	53.9%
1998	100%	74.9%	61.6%	72.6%	62.6%	53.1%
1999	100%	80.6%	61.6%	71.6%	65.0%	52.1%
2000	100%	78.2%	63.4%	72.2%	64.6%	52.8%

Source: National Committee on Pay Equity.

---

tt "Median Annual Earnings by Race and Sex" report – The National Committee on Pay Equity
tt Median annual earnings of black men and women, Hispanic men and women, and white women as a percentage of white men's median annual earnings

There are several Web sites that provide more specific salary matches for your profession. Since money does matter, find out how much you are likely to be paid. A good site to check out is **www.salary.com.** The information on this site empowers individuals and managers with the data needed to achieve a win-win situation in the compensation package.

Another helpful Web site is **www.wageweb.com.** This company offers an on-line salary service that provides information on over 170 benchmark positions. Or, go to **www.salarysource.com** to receive at least three different survey sources for every position you're considering. According to the Salary Source Web site, "Salary Source allows you to specify what base city you want to regionalize your data for among more than several thousand choices in the United States and U.S. Territories."

While salary should never be the main determining factor in choosing a career, it is necessary to do your homework. Be aware of your potential salary and consider the type of lifestyle you will be able to maintain given your earning potential.

To get a real grip on realty try out this great interactive survey by Jump$tart called "Reality Check," This site allows you to see exactly how much money you'll need to make to live the lifestyle you have in mind. To complete the survey type the following URL in your favorite web browser: **http://www.youngbiz.com/aspindex.asp?fileName =money_smartz/yb_money_smartz.htm** or visit **www.cdcresources.com** and click the "Reality Check" link.

Remember, it's not how much you make but how much you keep. Revisit the chart in the Money section and see why you can't afford not to save.

> *Remember, it's not how much you make but how much you keep.*

15

THE DRIVERS SEAT: HOW TO MAKE THE BEST CAREER CHOICES

By far, for me, the best career advice I received was to be open and take a "test drive." Applying for and participating in internships was the best way for me to narrow the field that I wanted to make my mark in.

When choosing a career and please be honest with yourself; consider the fact that the choice you make will be a part of you for many years. Don't take it lightly. Certainly don't pick it based on how much money you'll potentially make. Money is only one of many factors to weigh. For more guided assistance in choosing a career visit **www.mapping-your-future.org/planning.**

Follow your passion for the hallways are littered with bitter souls who choose the wrong profession for the wrong reason. You will have to pay your dues, you will have to prove yourself, and you will have to fight to be noticed. The process will be long and sometimes hard. It may take you a few positions before finding the perfect fit but, remembering why you choose a particular career path will be necessary to press on. Choose well.

There are so many resources for making good career choices. Here are some that I found useful:

The Pathfinder: How to Choose or Change Your Career for a Lifetime of Satisfaction and Success by Nicholas Lore — Through goal setting, list making, and other techniques, the book leads readers through the process of deciding exactly what they want to do for a living and finding a way to make it happen. It provides individualized advice to suit different temperaments and decision-making methods.

www.assessmentspecialists.com — Learn what you can succeed at and be successful! Career Coaches will match your natural abilities, interests, and personality to over 200 careers of today!

www.hotjobs.com — Provides a highly resourceful and dynamic exchange between opportunity seekers and employers. For opportunity seekers, HotJobs.com is a one-stop career resource center that offers advanced privacy features, numerous career tools, as well as, a comprehensive relocation center.

www.monster.com — A career network providing continuous access to the most progressive companies, as well as interactive, personalized tools to make the process effective and convenient. Features include a personal career management office; resume management, a personal job search agent, chats and message boards, privacy options, expert advice on job-seeking, and free newsletters.

Major in Success: Make College Easier, Fire Up Your Dreams, and Get a Very Cool Job by Patrick Combs — This book shows how absolutely any student can turn their studies into a major in success.

The book includes tips on how to get an internship that will knock the socks off future employers, inside information on which classes will put you on the fast track to career success, how to turn extracurricular activities into resume gold, and more.

College Grad Job Hunter: Insider Techniques and Tactics for Finding a Top-Paying Entry Level Job by Brian D. Krueger — This book packs 200-plus techniques and tactics, any one of which will make a significant impact on a job search. No theory. No philosophy. Just down to earth information a college grad can use immediately in their job search.

Naked at the Interview: Tips and Quizzes to Prepare You for Your First Real Job by Burton Jay Nadler. Each chapter begins with a quiz, followed by typical questions, action steps, and helpful resources. Coverage includes job search survival, career vocabulary, interviewing, and how to study for and ace interviews.

Best Jobs for the 21st Century for College Graduates by Michael J. Farr and LaVerne L. Ludden — Entries are arranged alphabetically and in lists according to categories, such as jobs with highest pay, best jobs for different types of workers, jobs based on levels of education and experience, and jobs based on interests.

From College to Career: Winning Resumes for College Graduates by Nancy Schuman and Adele Lewis — Offers help on "how to successfully emphasize your college courses, internships, computer skills, and work experience to gain a prospective employer's interest."

www.careerresource.com — Get career advice, find a mentor in your field of interest, and get on the fast track to career advancement with proven tips and techniques.

www.futuresteps.com — Helps people make the best career choices with career advice, guidance and information. Get help choosing a job, or finding the right training and education courses.

www.aftercollege.com — This is a free service for college students, job seekers, and recent graduates who are looking for jobs and internships. Post your resume and receive invitations from employers, or search for jobs at over 1,000 top companies.

www.howtointerview.com — A free resource for budding jobseekers and would-be interviewees. Our aim is to help you improve your interview skills thus helping you achieve that dream job.

www.jobvault.com — The Internet's ultimate destination for insider company information, advice, and career management services. Fortune recently called Vault "The best place on the Web to prepare for a job search."

www.jobthing.com — Get specialized information to help you land a job, develop your career and stay informed about employment trends in your industry.

16

THE ROAD LESS TRAVELED: IS ENTREPRENEURSHIP FOR YOU?

Are you considering taking the entrepreneurship route? It's not for everyone, but there are some strong arguments for taking the road less traveled. According to the National Association for the Self-Employed, entrepreneurs are smarter than the average American. Self-employed American's with bachelor's degrees and PhDs out pace the overall population by 7.6%, and 4.7% respectively.

When I founded my company in 1997, I was still employed. However, I started my business and worked weekends and nights to get it up and running. I had no formal training in running a business. But my knowledge and experience pushed my desire to help young adults avoid the landmines that left me debt laden and depressed. I also had the moral support of friends and family and a passion for knowledge. I read a lot to become familiar with how to start a business.

Most small business owners begin this way, however it is difficult to earn a living initially so good planning is key to future success. If business ownership is in your future, be sure to know what you're getting into. It is not to be taken lightly; it requires a tremendous amount of work.

Many business owners opt to work for someone else and gain the knowledge of how business works before venturing into entrepreneurship. In fact, most small business owners recommend this route.

Very little beats experience. But don't allow a lack of experience or age to keep you from pursuing your dream of being your own boss. Besides, enthusiasm and determination are also main ingredients in the success of a small business. The late Arthur Ashe, a stellar tennis player and the first black member of the U.S. Davis Cup team, put it best when he said, "Start where you are, use what you have, do what you can!"

There are several books and Web sites available to help you make an informed decision. Here are some that I found helpful:

The Young Entrepreneur's Edge by Jennifer Kushnell — How to transform your big idea into a thriving business.

www.youngandsuccessful.com — Supports the needs of young people from around the world as they attempt to build and thrive in both their personal and professional lives.

If You Want To Be Happy & Rich Don't Go To School by Robert Kiyosaki — Learn attitudes and abilities that will help you not merely to survive, but to prosper, regardless of whether the economy goes up or goes down.

www.sife.org — Students in Free Enterprise (SIFE) is the world's preeminent collegiate free enterprise organization. SIFE provides leadership training, regional competitions and career opportunity fairs for thousands of college students.

www.independentmeans.com — IMI has taken a hip and fresh approach to economic education and information for the Y-Generation audience. They are the first stop for news and expertise on starting a business, making, saving, giving and growing money.

www.nfte.com — The National Foundation for Teaching Entrepreneurship's (NFTE, pronounced "nifty") mission is to teach entrepreneurship education to low-income young people, ages 11 through 18, so they can become economically productive members of society by improving their academic, business, and technology and life skills.

www.youngentrepreneur.com — Seeks to establish and maintain a unique position among member-based communities online as being the most comprehensive source for Young Entrepreneurs and new business start-ups.

The Quest for Capital: A Financing Guide for Entrepreneurs by Dee Power and Brian Hill — A practical guide to finance any business. Lack of funding is one of the main reasons why businesses fail. Don't let it happen to you. Get your company the money it needs to succeed.

www.realm.net — Is a place you can turn to for strategies, opportunities and connections to make your passion your way of life.

www.youngmoney.com — Young Money's mission is to take a historically complicated subject: Money Management, and make it fun and easy to understand. This is not Money Management 101. We know not everyone's majoring in finance, and that's okay.

www.bizmove.com — Providers of free small business guides, tips, techniques and general information.

Generation, Inc: The 100 Best Businesses for Young Entrepreneurs by Elina & Leah Furman — Shows you what you need to succeed in one hundred carefully selected start-ups—from low-cost options based on your special talent to high-end, think-big concepts.

What No One Ever Tells You About Starting Your Own Business : Real Life Start-Up Advice from 101 Successful Entrepreneurs by Jan Norman — Using more than 100 interviews with seasoned entrepreneurs, the author guides you through every stage of business start-up-from planning to marketing — and provides eye-opening lessons from successful business owners who've learned the hard way.

Free Money from the Federal Government for Small Businesses and Entrepreneurs by Laurie Blum —This book tells entrepreneurs how to tap into the hundreds of millions of dollars in government funding available to help start up or expand a small business. Includes complete addresses, phone and fax numbers, and contact names.

The McGraw-Hill Guide to Starting Your Own Business: A Step-by-Step Blueprint for the First Time Entrepreneur by Stephen C. Harper — This step-by-step guide shows new and prospective business owners how to beat the odds and join the select few who follow their dreams to financial reward, job satisfaction, and self reliance.

— • ::≡◆>0◁◆≡:: • —

18

CONCLUSION

I wish I had a book like this when I was in college. My inspiration for sharing my life experiences and knowledge with you is a sincere desire that you will make different choices because of reading this book. I hope that you have been helped by what you've read.

A wise woman once told me, "You already have everything within you to succeed." I gave myself permission to believe that and I challenge you to do the same. Success is not without its mistakes, in fact, failure is a necessary part of success. It's not how many times you fall down — rather how many times you get back up that will determine your success. Sometimes you have to walk through the valley before you reach your mountaintop.

Be observant. Choose wisely. Learn from others' mistakes. Ignorance is not bliss so be sure to keep your eyes open along the way. Embrace knowledge, fiercely guard truth, fight for justice, be curious, and love like you'll never get hurt.

Whether you decide to climb the ladder of Corporate America or venture down the road less traveled, "Go confidently in the direction of your dreams. Live the life you've always imagined." Thoreau

— • ::━╡◆⊃◑€◆╪━:: • —

19

RESOURCES

Leaders are readers, never stop learning, growing and applying your knowledge. Use the following resources to make informed decisions about money, love, and the dream job.

For quick access to any of the resources offered below, visit **www.cdcresources.com** for active links to the information you're looking for.

Books   on   Money

How I Retired at 26! A step-by-step guide to accessing your FREEDOM and WEALTH at any age by Asha Tyson—This dynamic book will change the way you think about money and will shatter the barriers that keep you from reaching your full financial potential. It presents a no-nonsense success formula, no-fail financial strategy and an inspiration story of triumph.

The Wealthy Barber, by David Chilton. This book shows readers how to achieve the financial independence they've always dreamed of. With the help of his fictional barber, Roy, and a large dose of humor, Chilton encourages readers to take control of their financial future and build wealth slowly, steadily, and with sure success.

Learn to Earn: A Beginner's Guide to the Basics of Investing and Business by Peter Lynch, John Rothchild. This book is for beginning investors of all ages. Lynch and coauthor John Rothchild are family men who are worried that teenagers aren't learning enough about the importance of American companies in improving lives and creating wealth.

Talking Dollars and Making Sense: A Wealth Building Guide for African-Americans by Brooke Stevens — Offers prudent and sensitive advice on money management that will help readers take control of their finances and plan more effectively for the future, in a guide that offers a specific focus on the African-American experience.

Rich Dad, Poor Dad: What the Rich Teach Their Kids About Money that the Poor and Middle Class Do   Not! by Robert T. Kiyosaki, Sharon L. Lechter. This book compellingly advocates the type of "financial literacy" that's never taught in schools. He references his highly educated but fiscally unstable father, and the multimillionaire eighth-grade dropout father of his closest friend. The lifelong monetary problems experienced by his "poor dad" (whose weekly paychecks, while respectable, were never sufficient to meet family needs) pounded home the counterpoint communicated by his "rich dad"— that the poor and the middle class work for money, but the rich have money work for them. It explains how to acquire assets so that the jobs can eventually be shed.

Think and Grow Rich by Napoleon Hill — A classic and must read for anyone looking to elevate their station in life. Napoleon Hill's philosophy teaches you how to recognize, relate, assimilate and apply principles whereby you can achieve any goal whatsoever that doesn't violate Universal Law Books on Love

The Road Less Traveled: A New Psychology of Love, Traditional Values and Spiritual Growth by M. Scott Peck — In this guide to confronting and resolving our problems-and suffering through the changes-we learn that we can reach a higher level of self-knowledge. This book can help you learn the very nature of loving relationships; how to recognize true compatibility; how to distinguish dependency from love; how to become one's own person; how to be a more sensitive person.

Keeping the Love You Find: A Guide for Singles by Harville Hendrix — A guide to holding onto love shows readers how to meet the challenges of a new relationship, avoid making the same mistakes, deal with emotional issues, and improve their odds.

Dating for Dummies by Dr. Joy Browne — Addresses those complexities of dating. Exactly how do you meet a potential date? How do you present yourself in the most favorable light? How do you negotiate that first date? And, how do you proceed from there? The process still comes down to chemistry, but Browne shows how many ways there are to make sure you get your best possible chance with Mr./Ms. Right.

Mars and Venus on a Date: A Guide for Navigating the 5 Stages of Dating to Create a Loving and Lasting Relationship by John Gray — Gray identifies the five stages in the dating process: attraction, uncertainty, exclusivity, intimacy and engagement. He carefully describes the benefits and pitfalls of each of these stages, leading to a better understanding of a relationship's true potential.

Books on Finding the Dream Job

Love Is The Killer App: How To Win Business and Influence Friends by Tim Sanders — Love in a business context means sharing your compassion, your knowledge, and your network with people you want to do business with. It's also about the hard work of creating value in yourself by reading everything in your field and looking for any opportunities to share your knowledge. Read this book and find out how to become a love cat—a nice, smart person who succeeds in business and in life. Here's the real scoop: Nice guys don't finish last. They rule!

From College to the Real World: Street-Smart Strategies for Landing Your Dream Job and Creating a Successful Future by James Malinchak— A must read for every college student! This book teaches students how to separate themselves from the crowd so they can beat out any candidate for any position. The strategies in this book have one objective: TO GET STUDENTS HIRED!

The Pathfinder : How to Choose or Change Your Career for a Lifetime of Satisfaction and Success by Nicholas Lore— Through goal setting, list making, and other techniques, the book leads readers though the process of deciding exactly what they want to do for a living and finding a way to make it happen. It provides individualized advice to suit different temperaments and decision-making methods.

Major in Success: Make College Easier, Fire Up Your Dreams, and Get a Very Cool Job by Patrick Combs — This book shows how absolutely any student can turn their studies into a major in success. Includes tips on how to get an internship that will knock the socks off future employers, inside info on which classes will put you on the fast track to career success, how to turn extracurricular activities into resume gold, and more.

College Grad Job Hunter: Insider Techniques and Tactics for Finding a Top-Paying Entry Level Job by Brian D. Krueger — This book packs over 200 techniques and tactics, any one of which will make a significant impact on a job search. No theory. No philosophy. Just down to earth information a college grad can use immediately in their job search.

Naked At The Interview: Tips and Quizzes to Prepare You for Your First Real Job by Burton Jay Nadler — Each chapter begins with a quiz, followed by typical questions, action steps and helpful resources. Coverage includes job search survival, career vocabulary, interviewing, and how to study for and ace interviews.

Best Jobs for the 21st Century for College Graduates by Michael J. Farr and LaVerne L. Ludden — Entries are arranged alphabetically, and in lists according to categories such as jobs with highest pay, best jobs for different types of workers, jobs based on levels of education and experience, and jobs based on interests

From College to Career: Winning Resumes for College Graduates by Nancy Schuman and Adele Lewis — How to emphasize your college courses, internships, computer skills, and work experience to gain a prospective employer's interest.

The Young Entrepreneur's Edge by Jennifer Kushnell — How to transform your big idea into a thriving business.

If You Want To Be Happy & Rich Don't Go To School by Robert Kiyosaki — Learn attitudes and abilities that will help you not merely to survive, but to prosper, regardless of whether the economy goes up or goes down.

The Quest for Capital: A Financing Guide For Entrepreneurs by Dee Power and Brian Hill — A practical guide to finance any business. Lack of funding is one of the main reasons why businesses fail. Don't let it happen to you. Get your company the money it needs to succeed.

Generation, Inc: The 100 Best Businesses for Young Entrepreneurs by Elina & Leah Furman — Shows you what you need to succeed in one hundred carefully selected start-ups—from low-cost options based on your special talent to high-end, think-big concepts.

What No One Ever Tells You About Starting Your Own Business: Real Life Start-Up Advice from 101 Successful Entrepreneurs by Jan Norman — Using more than 100 interviews with seasoned entrepreneurs, the author guides you through every stage of business start-up-from planning to marketing — & provides eye-opening lessons from successful business owners who've learned the hard way.

Free Money from the Federal Government for Small Businesses and Entrepreneurs by Laurie Blum — This book tells entrepreneurs how to tap into the hundreds of millions of dollars in government funding available to help start up or expand a small business. Includes complete addresses, phone and fax numbers, and contact names.

Web Sites on Money

www.youngmoney.com — Young Money's mission is to take a historically complicated subject: Money Management, and make it fun and easy to understand. This is not Money Management 101. We know not everyone's majoring in finance, and that's okay.

www.aboutchecking.com — An educational Web site that contains all you need to know about managing a checking account. Don't miss the interactive training demos, called Checkbook Basics, that teach important skills, including how to fill out checks, registers, and how to balance your account. Now learning the basics of managing a checkbook is easy, interactive and fun!

www.credit-card-application-store.com — Here you will find the best credit card offers from the internet. Just use the directory to see reviews of and links to the credit card companies offering secured and unsecured credit cards. You can apply for a Platinum, Diamond, Titanium, Gold or Classic Visa or fill out an application for a secured MasterCard. Whether you are looking to apply for a Visa, MasterCard or American Express Card, you will find the links you need to fill out an online application from the directory on the right.

www.chexhelp.com — The ChexSystems network is comprised of member banks and credit unions that regularly contribute information on mishandled checking and savings accounts to a central location. Member institutions share this information to help them assess the risk of opening new accounts. You may obtain a copy of your consumer report from this site.

www.independentmeans.com — IMI has taken a hip and fresh approach to economic education and information for the Y-Generation audience. They are the first stop for news and expertise on starting a business, making, saving, giving and growing money.

www.rightonthemoney.org — *Right on the Money!* is the national personal finance show, hosted by Chris Farrell helps you solve your own money problems and provides tools to help build your financial future. This is a great resource if you don't have access to the TV show.

www.cheapskatemonthly.com — Cheapskate Monthly is committed to helping you learn how to get out of debt and stay out — all on the money you earn right now. Even if you are living paycheck to paycheck, buried under a pile of horrible debt or just spinning your financial wheels, there is so much hope and help on this site.

www.fool.com — Motley Fool's goal is to "educate, amuse and enrich." The company is committed to using its voice to help those with money as well as those without it.

www.smartmoney.com — This highly interactive site picks up where the magazine (of the same name) leaves off. If you're your really ready to take control of your financial life this site will be a valuable resource.

Web Sites on Love

www.lovecalculator.com — Don't bank on the outcome, but it is fun to check it out. Doctor Love himself designed this site just for you. With The Love Calculator, you can calculate the probability on a successful relationship between two people. The Love Calculator is an *affective* way to get an impression of what the chances are on a relationship between certain people.

www.lifeway.com — Home of "True Love Waits" which challenges students to make the right and radical choice of sexual purity until marriage is a great resource for advice and information about the issues that young adults face about love and relationships.

www.love-n-kisses.com — Get advice, tips, recipes, and even poetry! This site strives to be a one-stop-shop for all things romantic.

www.lovexpress.com — If you're looking for tips, techniques, and ready-to-use material with which to express your love and affection to someone special in your life, you've come to the right place! Here, you'll find a mountain of romantic information that will help you communicate your innermost feelings.

www.dvirc.org.au/whenlove — What do you do when love hurts? Being in love is supposed to feel great. However, sometimes it just feels confusing. What can you do if you are being hurt, controlled or treated badly in a relationship?

Web Sites on Finding the Dream Job

www.assessmentspecialists.com — Learn what you can succeed at and be successful! Career Coaches will match your natural abilities, interests and personality to over 200 careers of today!

www.hotjobs.com — Provides a highly resourceful and dynamic exchange between opportunity seekers and employers. For opportunity seekers, HotJobs.com is a one-stop career resource center that offers advanced privacy features, numerous career tools, as well as a comprehensive relocation center.

www.monster.com — A career network, providing continuous access to the most progressive companies, as well as interactive, personalized tools to make the process effective and convenient. Features include a personal career management office; resume management, a personal job search agent, chats and message boards; privacy options; expert advice on job-seeking; and free newsletters.

www.careerresource.com — Get career advice, find a mentor in your field of interest, get on the fast track to career advancement with proven tips and techniques.

www.futuresteps.com — Helps people make the best career choices, with career advice, guidance and information. Get help choosing a job, or finding the right training and education courses.

www.aftercollege.com — Is a free service for college students, job seekers and recent graduates who are looking for jobs and internships. Post your resume and receive invitations from employers or search for jobs at over 1,000 top companies.

www.howtointerview.com — A free resource for budding jobseekers and would-be interviewees. Our aim is to help you improve your interview skills thus helping you achieve that dream job.

www.jobvault.com — The Internet's ultimate destination for insider company information, advice, and career management services. *Fortune* recently called Vault "The best place on the Web to prepare for a job search."

www.jobthing.com — Specialized information to help you land a job, develop your career and stay informed about employment trends in your industry

www.youngandsuccessful.com — Supports the needs of young people from around the world as they attempt to build and thrive in both their personal and professional lives.

www.sife.org — Students in Free Enterprise (SIFE) is the world's preeminent collegiate free enterprise organization. SIFE provides leadership training, regional competitions and career opportunity fairs for thousands of college students.

www.nfte.com — The National Foundation for Teaching Entrepreneurship's (NFTE, pronounced "nifty") mission is to teach entrepreneurship education to low-income young people, ages 11 through 18, so they can become economically productive members of society by improving their academic, business, and technology and life skills.

www.youngentrepreneur.com — Seeks to establish and maintain a unique position among member-based communities online as being the most comprehensive source for Young Entrepreneurs and new business start-ups.

www.realm.net — Is a place you can turn to for strategies, opportunities and connections to make your passion your way of life.

www.bizmove.com — Provides free small business guides, tips, techniques and general information.

www.youngbiz.com — Is all about the business of being young. A teenager makes tons of decisions every day; decisions that can be as small as what cereal to have for breakfast to which college you want to attend. We're here to take those awesome decision-making skills and use them to make great financial and business decisions. Every day you'll find articles, profiles, interviews, and letters dealing with everything you need to know about being young and in control of all of the crazy parts of your life.

Additional Resources

- **www.textbookhound.com** — Compares prices for college textbooks. It even allows you to enter a search for multiple books at once. Best of all, books are listed according to the lowest price. "Release the hound . . ."**Reference Directory:**

- **The Millionaire Next Door**, by Thomas J. Stanley, Ph.D. and William D. Danko, Ph. D. Pocket Books, 1996

- **Credit Card Nation: The Consequences of America's Addiction to Credit**, by Robert D. Manning. Basic Books, 2000

- **Fair Credit Reporting Act** Public Law 107-56, October 2001

- **The Federal Trade Commission** Form OMB#3084-0047 or visit https://rn.ftc.gov/dod/wsolcq$.startup?Z_ORG _CODE=PU01